The
Catholic Girl's Survival Guide
for the Single Years

The
Catholic Girl's Survival Guide
for the Single Years

The Nuts and Bolts of Staying Sane and Happy While Waiting for Mr. Right

by Emily Stimpson

EMMAUS
ROAD
PUBLISHING

Steubenville, Ohio
www.emmausroad.org

Emmaus Road Publishing
1468 Parkview Circle
Steubenville, Ohio 43952

Library of Congress Control Number: 2011945595
ISBN: 9781937155346

Cover design and layout by
Theresa Westling

Cover and inside artwork:
Lindsay Carpenter

Table of Contents

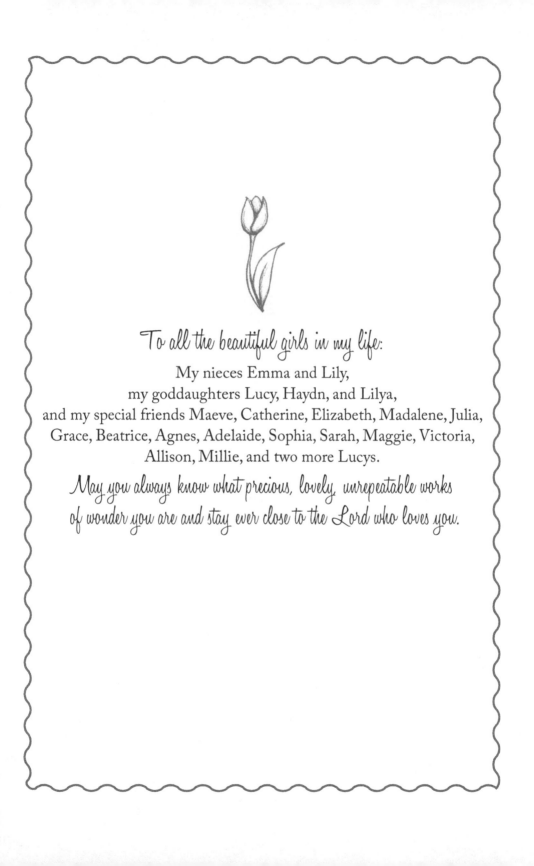

To all the beautiful girls in my life:

My nieces Emma and Lily,
my goddaughters Lucy, Haydn, and Lilya,
and my special friends Maeve, Catherine, Elizabeth, Madalene, Julia,
Grace, Beatrice, Agnes, Adelaide, Sophia, Sarah, Maggie, Victoria,
Allison, Millie, and two more Lucys.

May you always know what precious, lovely, unrepeatable works
of wonder you are and stay ever close to the Lord who loves you.

Everything the Catholic Single Girl
Needs to Know About . . .
This Book

On my twenty-seventh birthday, my very married friend Susanne sent me a book. It was called *Embracing Your Single Vocation* (or something to that effect). My first reaction, upon opening the package, was to burst into tears.

Then I read a couple pages.

I cried even harder.

The hateful thing was all about bucking up and being happy about your husbandless state, accepting the fact that, since no wedding ring was in view, God was probably calling you to be alone forever and ever and ever, and, above all, recognizing how jolly that could be.

Ten pages into the book I threw it in the trash and called Susanne.

"This is the worst birthday present anyone has ever given me," I sobbed into the phone. "I'm only twenty-seven. I have lots of time to get married. What were you thinking?"

I don't remember her reply. I was too busy crying. Something about trying to be helpful I suppose. Before the conversation ended, however,

I do know that I extracted from her a promise to never give that book to another woman again. As far as I know, she's honored that promise.

I have a promise to make as well.

I promise you this book is not that book.

If some well-meaning married friend, relative, or, heaven forbid, parent has given this to you, don't worry—I won't in any way, shape, or form tell you to buck up and be happy about being single forever and ever. Just because you're single at twenty-five, thirty-five, or even fifty-five is no reason to believe you're destined for spinsterhood. My hope for you is that you're not single forever and ever. I hope you meet Prince Charming tomorrow if that's your heart's desire.

But if he's anything like my dawdling Prince Charming, there might be some waiting involved. Which, I'm afraid, is why I am going to tell you to buck up and be happy.

Before you throw this book in the trash, hear me out.

Despite how it may seem, the years you and I spend waiting for toddlers to chase or husbands to feed don't have to be years of woe and misery. Yes, the waters in which singles sail are undeniably choppy and the winds wicked strong. But, at times, the sea of the single life can actually be much calmer and more pleasant than the sea of married life.

I guess you've heard that before. Maybe you're not buying. Trust me, in many ways I'm with you. The single years have their pluses, but when weighed against the softness of a newborn's skin or the strength of a man's arms, those pluses rarely add up.

Nevertheless, husbands can't be conjured out of thin air. Nor can they be prayed into existence. If that were the case I would have one by now. No, God sends them along in his own good time, and until then, those of us who believe our vocation is marriage have a choice. We can happily do our best to make the most of our time sans spouse. Or we can sulk.

Most of us, admittedly, will do our fair share of both. And there will be days, months—years even—when there's a whole lot more sulking than smiling going on. But again, it is possible to keep those times to a minimum. You just have to know a few tricks of the trade . . . tricks that go beyond an encyclopedic knowledge of husband-hunting novenas.

Those tricks are what this little book is all about. It's chock-full of unsolicited, unvarnished, and eminently practical advice on the nitty gritty "how-to" of the single years: dating, the biological clock, finances, married people, their children, depression, and more. It's about everything (or almost everything) that you, as a single Catholic woman, need to know. If Susanne had given me this book eight years ago, I swear I wouldn't have thrown it in the trash . . . at least not after the first ten pages.

Before we go any further, however, a few notes on that advice.

First, although much of the counsel this book contains is applicable for divorced, annulled, or young widowed Catholics, I'm writing as a single, never-been-married Catholic, so it's single, never-been-married Catholics that this book primarily addresses.

That's the situation I know. It's what I understand. I would be loathe to say something stupid or foolish about the struggles of divorced, annulled, or widowed Catholics when I know so very little about the unique challenges they face. Nevertheless, I hope those of you in a different situation from mine still read on. Feel free to curse me roundly when I'm not addressing the struggles on your plate. I don't mind.

The same goes for women still discerning their vocation. (Not the cursing part. The reading part.) I'm assuming most of the women reading this are reasonably certain God is calling them to the vocation of marriage, so it's to them that most of the advice is targeted. Nevertheless, even if your final destination is a convent in Tennessee or a community of consecrated singles in Maryland, for now you're pretty much in the same boat as those of us desiring marriage, so again, read on. Take what applies to you. Leave the rest.

Those who should not read on, however, are men. This book is called *The Catholic **Girl's** Survival Guide for the Single Years* for a reason. It's meant for girls, not boys, and I'm afraid men will be horribly disappointed and bored by everything beyond Chapter One or so. I know, Dear Reader, if you are a man, I can't stop you from reading this book. But when all my talk about babies and beauty and cashmere sweaters leaves you feeling disoriented or disturbed, don't blame me. I warned you.

Finally, please don't suffer any illusions that I think being single is easy or that I'm even all that good at following my own advice. I don't, and I'm not. In many ways, I think I'm writing this book as much for me as for anyone. Perhaps more for me than anyone. At thirty-five, I'm not supposed to be single. I'm supposed to have a minimum of five kids by now, with more on the way. That was always the plan, my plan that is, and the fact that it hasn't worked out is a constant source of heartache and heartbreak. I'm daily trying to come to grips with it and understand why there's no husband or babies on the immediate horizon. This book is one way I'm doing that. That's how you figure things out when you're a writer, you see. You write about them.

That being said, I am still far more happy than not and somewhat more sane than not. Those are slim qualifications for penning a tome on the single years, but qualifications nonetheless. The truth is, I'm increasingly surprised by how good my lot in a husband-free life is, how little cause I have for complaint, and how ridiculously generous God is with the blessings he dishes out. He is loveliness itself, and the deeper I dive into his life, the more bearable this whole single thing gets.

But I'm jumping ahead of myself. That sort of talk is for the last chapter. Right now, we have other fish to fry . . . starting with: Why on earth are we still single?

Everything the Catholic Single Girl
Needs to Know About . . .

Vocations and the Single Life

A s I said, first things first. Before we dive into dating, men, and other disasters, there are a few important questions we need to settle, like . . . What the heck is going on here? Why are we still single? And why do people keep calling it a vocation?

Let's start with what we're doing, something which in common parlance is currently called "The Single Life."

The good news about what we're doing (in one way) is that we're not doing it alone.

According to the most recent data from the U.S. Census Bureau, a grand total of 96 million unmarried people now live in the United States. That's 43 percent of adults over the age of eighteen. Many of those folks are divorced (24 percent). Some are widowed (15 percent). But the bulk (61 percent) have never walked down the aisle.[1]

---

1 "Single? You're Not Alone," *CNN.com*, August 19, 2010. Available at http://articles.cnn.com/2010-08-19/living/single.in.america_1_single-fathers-single-mothers-single-parents?_s=PM:LIVING.

When it comes to Catholics specifically, the Center for Applied Research in the Apostolate reports that 6.9 million Catholic men and 6.1 million Catholic women have never been married. That's a lot of unmarried Catholics. And with the number of Catholic marriages dropping every year, the number of Catholic singles doesn't seem likely to fall anytime soon.[2]

Again, we're not in this alone. There are lots of others in the same boat as you and I. And as long as you set aside the long-term consequences of population implosion, widespread loneliness and depression, children growing up in unstable homes, aging adults with no family to care for them, the rampant sexual immorality common among most singles, and the breakdown of civil society as we know it, that's the good news.

So what's the bad news?

The bad news is that nobody really knows what the heck we're doing. We're sailing in uncharted waters.

Never before in history have quite so many people delayed marriage quite so late into adulthood. Some delay by choice. Others by chance. Nonetheless, marriage is delayed for a whole lot of us.

And that's not normal.

Stay your protests. I hear them. How does the single life qualify, in any way, as "uncharted"? After all, haven't people lived the single life since time immemorial?

The answer is yes . . . and no.

The Single Life Through the Ages

Virgin Martyrs and Spinster Aunts

For however many years the Earth has danced around the sun, there have, of course, been men and women who, for various reasons, never married. There were unwedded individuals. They were, however, few in number, they didn't call themselves "singles," and the lifestyle they lived bore no resemblance to the lifestyle we call "The Single Life."

In fact, until Christianity came around, the unmarried state was generally considered an aberration, a fate to be avoided at any cost, especially for

---

2 "Catholic Singles Feel Angst," *The Washington Times*, Nov. 20, 2008. Available at http://www.washington-times.com/news/2008/nov/20/keeping-faith-in-dating/.

women. Sure, you had the occasional celibates like the Essenes at Qumran. But the general public thought those folks a bit odd. The thing to do, culture after culture insisted, was to marry and marry young.

Then, along came Jesus. That changed things.

Before you could say "St. Paul's First Letter to the Corinthians," all sorts of men and women were throwing themselves into the lion's jaws rather than the marriage bed. They took the apostle's endorsement of singleness seriously and were convinced that if they wanted to be good Christians, they needed to eschew marital love.

They also, however, thought Jesus would materialize on the horizon any day.

As soon as Christians realized that the eschaton might be somewhat less imminent, the situation stabilized. Lots of nice Catholic girls and boys decided that they didn't have to choose between marriage and death. Virginity wasn't their only option.

Some Christians, of course, still chose virginity or celibacy. They took holy orders or headed off to the convent, vowing the whole of their lives, body and soul, to Christ. A precious few also chose to make those vows but live them outside the monastery's walls. They lived at home (à la St. Catherine of Siena) or walled themselves up in little buildings attached to churches (think of anchoresses such as Julian of Norwich). Some also headed off to the desert (Anthony of Egypt) or built hermitages in the mountains of France (St. Emilion).

And everyone who didn't become a priest, enter a convent, or set up house in a cave?

Well, as before, they got married.

Again, there were exceptions. There were spinster aunts and bachelor uncles. There were sweet old maids who cherished the memory of The One That Got Away, and there were funny old men who ran from women like mice from cats.

But they weren't the norm.

Now they are. Now we are.

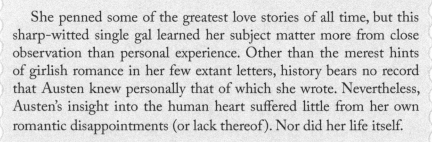

Hip Spinster Sisters in History, Episode One:

Jane Austen

She penned some of the greatest love stories of all time, but this sharp-witted single gal learned her subject matter more from close observation than personal experience. Other than the merest hints of girlish romance in her few extant letters, history bears no record that Austen knew personally that of which she wrote. Nevertheless, Austen's insight into the human heart suffered little from her own romantic disappointments (or lack thereof). Nor did her life itself.

By all accounts her forty-one years as a single woman were full and happy ones, made not only bearable but actually enjoyable by a mind livelier than any Parisian café and a capacity for conversation more stimulating than a cup of cappuccino. Austen knew intimately what Mr. Knightley meant when he told the capricious Emma, "A mind lively and at ease, can do with seeing nothing, and can see nothing that does not answer."

Commitment-Phobes, Cohabitators, and Christians

Few of us, however, bear a close resemblance to those spinster aunts and bachelor uncles of old.

We're not, for example, living quietly at home with our parents or being shuffled between much put upon nieces and nephews. We women folk actually get to do things like go to school, hold a profession, and read books without causing undue scandal. We're not treated like children well into our dotage. All of which is to the good.

Other elements of today's single life, however, are less to the good.

Generally speaking (which I know is somewhat dangerous but necessary nonetheless), unmarried individuals today can be subdivided into two categories.

First, there's the single majority. These folks live their single life according to the dictates of the media and culture, taking their cues from episodes of *Jersey Shore* or *How I Met Your Mother*. Which is to say that, to them, being single does not necessitate chastity. Almost the opposite, in fact.

Sociologists and statisticians tell us that members of this group typically have their first sexual encounter sometime in high school, then engage in a half dozen or more intense, intimate, and exclusive relationships with members of the opposite sex throughout their teens and twenties. By their early twenties, at least a quarter of these singles are living with one of those partners. Sometimes those relationships culminate in marriage. Most of the time they don't. Couples break up, move on, and eventually move in with other sexual partners. And the cycle continues, sexual license resulting from, as much as it leads to, enduring singleness.[3]

That's one category. The other category is us, the minority—nice Christian girls (and boys), some perhaps who made mistakes in the past, but who nonetheless are determined not to make those mistakes again. We're not sleeping around. We're not sleeping with anyone. And we're certainly not shacking up with anyone. But we're also not getting married.

We would like to. We'd really like to. But it's not happening. We date. We sign up for Catholic Match. We go to speed dating nights at our parish. But that right person never comes along. Or if he does, something's wrong. He can't commit. He can't decide. He's still discerning his vocation. You know the excuses. They're a little different from the excuses the general population gives, but the end result is the same. And it doesn't involve a wedding ring.

The two categories aren't, of course, entirely separate. Sin and grace mean some folks move out of one category and into another. When the move is from the unchaste majority into the chaste minority, those doing the moving usually bring a whole lot of baggage with them. Guilt, broken hearts, wounds from habitual sin and past relationships—that all takes its toll, and often gets in the way of a person entering into a healthy and committed relationship (or the priesthood or consecrated life, if that's where they're supposed to end up).

There also, unfortunately, are quite a few moves in the opposite direction. Chastity is hard. Finding a good Christian boy or girl is hard. Living the Christian life is hard. Temptation is indeed tempting. So people fall. And the number of eligible potential spouses for the minority grows smaller still.

---

3 See for example "Facts on American Teens Sexual and Reproductive Health" compiled by the Guttmacher Institute and published in January 2011. Available at http://www.guttmacher.org/pubs/FB-ATSRH.html.

For all those reasons and more, women like you and me find ourselves reluctantly single later—maybe much later—than we'd like. It's not how we would have charted things out. And the Church understands that. She feels for us.

But she's not quite sure what to do with us.

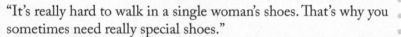

Bad Show. Great Quote.

"It's really hard to walk in a single woman's shoes. That's why you sometimes need really special shoes."

—*Sex and the City*

The Single Vocation?

One response opted for by many priests, some bishops, and lots of well-intentioned married folks, is to try to console unwedded Catholics by singing the praises of the single vocation. They talk about all the good single people can do, all the different ways we can make gifts of ourselves, and all the opportunities open to us because of our singleness.

They mean well. But all that talk brings little consolation. For most, it doesn't ring true. That may have something to do with the fact that even the people using the term "single vocation" don't always know what it means. It's a term they've pulled from their Catholic lexicon without ever stopping to consider its definition. Others use it imprecisely. They don't clarify the term in context.

Both problems stem from the fact that the whole idea of the unconsecrated single life as a vocation is rather a novelty . . . at least in the sense that well-meaning Catholics use the term today, as something akin to the vocation of marriage or holy orders. In fact, it's not mentioned anywhere in magisterial teaching. Not in any encyclicals. Not in any apostolic exhortations. And not in the Catechism.

The Church, not surprisingly, has acknowledged that single people exist. It would be rather hard to ignore that fact. We even get a shout out in Paragraph 1658 of the Catechism. That, however, is the section dealing with the vocation of marriage, and the paragraph basically tells pastors and married couples to remember us and take pity on us. It doesn't equate the unconsecrated single state in life with a vocation akin to marriage. And that's for good reason.

The Catechism's Take

"We must also remember the great number of *single persons* who, because of the particular circumstances in which they have to live—often not of their choosing—are especially close to Jesus' heart and therefore deserve the special affection and active solicitude of the Church, especially of pastors. Many remain *without a human family* often due to conditions of poverty. Some live their situation in the spirit of the Beatitudes, serving God and neighbor in exemplary fashion. The doors of homes, the 'domestic churches,' and of the great family which is the Church must be open to all of them."

—*Catechism of the Catholic Church*, no. 1658

A Vocational Primer

Before we go any further, let's make sure we're not likewise throwing our terms around willy nilly. When the Church talks about the word "vocation," what does she mean?

Sometimes, she means the journey or the path we're on—the journey to holiness. To holiness, God calls you, me, and every member of the human race. That's why this path is what's commonly referred to as the "universal vocation."

As the Catechism tells us, God created us to live in loving union with him for all eternity (CCC 772). A nuptial relationship with him is what we're meant for, what we were made for. So our vocation, our job, in this life, is to get where we're meant to go. Since holiness consists of being in a state of grace, and grace is mostly a God thing, the bulk of the work on this journey is done by God himself. Which is bully for us. We simply have to receive the grace God offers and do our best to make a gift of ourselves, in love, to him and others.

That's one meaning of vocation—the path we're on. The other is what we do on the path. That's our secondary vocation. It encompasses our nine to five occupations (butchers, bakers, candlestick makers) plus our various apostolic activities (singing in the Church choir, volunteering at the local crisis pregnancy clinic, bringing meals to shut-ins). It also can encompass the bearing of certain trials or situations in life. Think of people with serious or chronic illness who are often referred to as having a "vocation to suffering." That's a secondary vocation. It's something you do (or endure) that helps you in the journey to holiness.

There is, of course, one more meaning to the word "vocation," and it has to do with how, as adults, we travel down the path to God. That "how" is called our "primary vocation." Traditionally, the Church has identified three of these: Holy Orders, Marriage, and Consecrated Life. Holy Orders can mean the deaconate, but most commonly it just means the priesthood and episcopacy. Marriage means, well, marriage, the permanent union of one man and one woman. And consecrated life is the catchall phrase that applies to religious brothers and sisters, as well as lay people, like Opus Dei numeraries, who consecrate themselves to the Lord's service.

Each of those primary vocations is defined by the gift of self. The priest gives himself to Christ's Church. Married persons give themselves to a husband or wife. And consecrated persons give themselves directly to God: They start living now the relationship we're all called to live in eternity.

In the case of each primary vocation, that gift of self is not a transitory or temporary thing. It's not given one day and taken back the next. Rather, the central relationship of each is spousal. It's exclusive, total, and enduring. When the gift of self is made to God, enduring is a "for all eternity" kind of enduring. When the gift of self is made to another person, it's just an "until death do us part" kind of enduring. Nevertheless, the idea is the same: You fully and freely give yourself to another, and through that giving you pursue your universal vocation, holiness.

You also could say that through one spousal relationship you prepare yourself for another spousal relationship, the spousal relationship God calls you to enter into with himself. When considered in that light, a primary vocation isn't just "how" you journey to holiness. It's with whom you make the journey.

As for figuring out who your companion will be on the path to holiness—the Church, another person, or God himself—well, that's a question for prayer. But spiritual directors and those charged with helping people discern their vocation have long abided by the principle that if you have a strong and lasting desire for a certain vocation, a desire that's held up through years of prayer and discernment, you're most likely called to that vocation. That's because the primary vocation to which God calls you is the vocation he made you to desire. It's the vocation that helps you be more you, more the person God made you to be.

Vocation vo-ca-tion (noun) [vö káysh'n]

1. holiness. where you're going (*universal vocation*).
2. the spousal relationship with God, the Church, or another person that helps you get where you're going (*primary vocation*).
3. what you do as you journey towards your universal vocation, i.e., your work, your apostolate, your suffering (*secondary vocation*).

A Faux Vocation?

So where in all that does the much talked about "single vocation" fit? Is it even a real vocation at all?

That depends on what you mean by vocation.

If you're asking if it can be considered part of one's secondary vocation, then most definitely. Singleness can very much be a cross, a source of struggles and suffering offered up to God as you journey towards him. It's also an opportunity, however short or long-lived, to serve God and others in a unique way. It's definitely something you do on the path towards holiness.

But is *unconsecrated* singlehood a primary vocation? In some Catholic circles, the jury is still out on that. But it's hard to see how the answer can be anything other than no.

Remember, primary vocations are exclusive and enduring. Once you give yourself to another—God, the Church, a husband or wife—you can't give yourself to anyone else. Ever. Or, at least not without the intervention of death or a tribunal.

Yet that's not the case for unconsecrated singlehood. It's a state in life that's generally transitory and always, at least technically, easy to exit. In other words, you don't have to get a tribunal's permission to cease being single. You are supposed to cease being single. You are supposed to enter into a spousal relationship with someone—the Church, God, or another person. You were made for a spousal relationship, not just in eternity, but also in time. And your spousal relationship in time prepares you for your spousal relationship in eternity. It's what helps you complete the journey to holiness.

The Missed Vocation

In theory, that all makes sense. In reality, however, it gets a bit sticky. After all, what about all the people who never marry? What about all the men and women who wait for a spouse only to wait in vain? Or what about those who don't feel called to marriage, the priesthood, or a religious order? What about them? Surely they have a single vocation? Or did they get left out when vocational assignments were being dispensed?

These are some of the questions raised by those who believe the single vocation can be a primary vocation. They're good questions. People of good faith disagree on the answers. But those who use those questions to advocate for the idea of a primary vocation to the single life seem to forget a couple things.

First, some seem to forget that for those who don't feel called to marriage, the priesthood, or a religious order, there is another option: consecrated singlehood. Consecrated singles live the consecrated vocation in the world, either as part of a community of other consecrated individuals or alone, having made private vows to their bishop. You don't have to live in a monastery in order to give yourself to God. It's the norm, but it's not a prerequisite. In the end, it doesn't matter where one lives the consecrated vocation. What matters is the decision to give one's self exclusively and enduringly to God, to consecrate one's self entirely and forever to his service.

Along with forgetting about consecrated singlehood, some folks also seem to forget that, unfortunately, there is such a thing as a missed vocation, a vocation that should have been but wasn't.

Everybody has a vocation. But not everyone will necessarily enter into the vocation to which God calls them. Sometimes that happens because of illness or accident—because of the tragic realities of life in a fallen world. These days, more often than not, it happens because of the misuse of that thing called free will.

Consider, for example, the vocation of marriage.

As he does with all his human creations, God, in his wisdom and love, gave those of us called to the vocation of marriage the ability to choose for ourselves what we do, think, and believe. He made us autonomous creatures, not puppets or slaves. Which means he won't drag us kicking and screaming into anything, vocation or otherwise. That's a good thing. Unfortunately not all of us use our free will to do good things. Some actually use it to do quite bad things. Terrible mistakes are made and lasting wounds incurred, wounds that at times render the bearers incapable of giving (or reluctant to give) themselves in marriage.

The result of that is one person, and potentially two, unable to pursue the vocation to which they're called.

It's rotten. But it happens.

From the "I Couldn't Have Said It Better Myself" File:

"There are certainly not so many men of large fortune in the world, as there are pretty women to deserve them."

—Jane Austen, *Mansfield Park*

The Living Dead and the Walking Wounded

This phenomenon of missed vocations happened en masse a century ago when the Powers That Be in Europe used their free wills to get drawn into a hornet's nest of political entanglements and territorial squabbles that culminated in World War I. That in turn wiped out almost a generation of young men in England, France, Germany, and Belgium. Millions of men died, and millions of young women, most of whom had authentic vocations to marriage, were left without men to marry. And that was through no fault of their own. Their fiancés and potential fiancés had perished in the trenches of Verdun and Ypres.

Today, a different kind of war, a culture war, seems to have left large numbers of Christians in the same position.

Remember that first category of singles we talked about? They're the culture war's fatally or near fatally wounded. The sexual revolution, divorce, the breakdown of the family, abortion, contraception, pornography, cohabitation, even serial dating—all those things and more have spiritually wounded men and women in our world as seriously as mustard gas physically wounded England's soldiers in 1917. Fiancés and potential fiancés have again been crippled, in spirit if not in fact.

Because of that, some people never will enter the primary vocation for which they were made, the vocation that reflects the deepest desires of their heart. Others among us will find our vocation late, either because we need to heal or because we need to wait for our future spouse to heal. That means some of us won't necessarily get the big Catholic family of our dreams. We might not get any children at all.

That's the tragic reality with which we have to come to terms. It might not be your reality or mine. A husband might be waiting around the corner for you as soon as you finish this chapter. But it will be some people's reality. It will possibly be somebody you love's reality. And glossing over that reality by pretending the unconsecrated single life is a vocation just like marriage isn't helpful. It gives men and women who are avoiding God's call to marriage, the priesthood, or consecrated life an excuse to not answer that call. And those of us who truly believe we're called to marriage won't find lasting consolation in the idea. It doesn't make sense to us why everyone else gets called to a vocation that is the fulfillment of their heart's desires, while we're indefinitely stuck with a vocation of which we want no part.

I'm afraid all this talk about missed vocations and the walking wounded has been more than a little depressing. Sorry about that. Had to be done though. In order to keep our sanity about us, we need to understand what the heck is going on in our lives and see some of the reasons why.

But we mustn't dwell. We need to remain hopeful. We need to pray that God will send us a spouse. And we need to pursue the oceans of grace God provides to help us discover and overcome whatever wounds might be hampering our own ability to enter into a spousal relationship.

In other words, we mustn't label ourselves as a missed vocation just yet. It's not over until it's over, for anyone.

Above all, however, we need to strive to see our single years, for as long as they last, as an integral part of our secondary vocation. Husband or no husband, we're all on that journey towards holiness, and whether we're single until we're twenty-five, thirty-five, or sixty-five, the lack of a spouse does indeed afford us the opportunity to do certain things along the path that marriage, the priesthood, and consecrated life might not. Offering up loads of heartache is one thing. But it's not the only thing.

So take heart. Be of good cheer. And know that just because you're sailing in uncharted waters doesn't mean you're predestined to capsize. God is there. Grace is there. Even when no one and nothing else is. He's quite lovely like that.

Of course, he also expects you to be lovely as well. Which is why, while you're waiting to be pursued by Mr. Right, you need to do some pursuing of your own. You need to pursue authentic femininity.

Ask the Single Girl

Dear Single Girl,

I love my roommates, but the older I get the more I think I'd like a place of my own, a *roommate-free* place of my own. Is that wrong of me?

—Housemate in Hagerstown

Dear Housemate,

I think you're asking the wrong question. It's not about if it's wrong to long for roommate-free living (it's not). Rather, it's about if it's wise for you at this present moment.

I know roommates can be exhausting. Even the good ones. Living in the same space requires lots of delicate negotiations—who can eat what, who does what chores, who can have friends over when, who pays what bills, etc. Likewise, no matter how close you are to your roommates, there will be times when those negotiations break down. Tears follow. And those are never fun.

That, of course, is the best case scenario, with roommates you like. Having roommates you don't like or who don't like you can be a nightmare. Your home becomes a minefield. You're never sure where or when the next explosion will be. You just know there will be one.

It's those very difficulties, however, that make roommates (both the good and the bad) so important. All that rubbing up against each other wears down everyone's rough edges. You learn to be flexible, to accommodate habits and routines different from your own. You also come to know yourself better, what habits you need to change and what personality traits need some tempering, not to mention what habits and personality traits you can and cannot live with in others.

In the end, living with other women is some of the best possible preparation for marriage there is. You'll find adjusting to life with a husband much easier if you've already spent years adjusting to life with roommates. You'll also have more money in the bank. If the husband never comes, that money will still be there. So will the lessons you learned and the good times you had.

That being said, over time, all that adjusting to one new person after another can wear you out. So can saying goodbye to the roommates you love the most. Plus, if you end up buying your own place, you may not want the extra hassle of being a landlord to renters. For all those reasons and more, I said goodbye to my last roommate a few years ago. After fourteen years of sharing rooms, apartments and houses with more than fifty different women (what comes of living your entire adult life in transitory places like DC and college towns), I'd had enough. Whatever rough edges were left, I decided, my husband would just have to deal with.

Do I miss living with my best friends? Yes. Would it be nice to have a little extra money coming in every month? Sure. Do I feel like adjusting to one more person whom I am neither sleeping with nor giving birth to? No.

Those are the kinds of questions you need to ask yourself before saying *adios* to your housemates. Discern if it's affordable, safe, and realistic given your own personality and situation. Then, even if you decide that it is, wait. Live with those roommates just a little while longer. In the absence of a husband, they are your companions on the path to sainthood. Walk with them as long as you can.

Chapter Two

Everything the Catholic Single Girl
Needs to Know About . . .
Who She Is and Who She's Called to Be

I hate Roman women.

Okay, technically, I don't hate them. As a good Catholic girl I'm not supposed to hate anyone. I know that. But if I could, I would hate Roman women. They're everything the culture says women should be—impossibly thin, impossibly beautiful, and impossibly sexy.

Which also happens to be everything I'm not.

Like most Americans, I don't do feminine the way Italian women do feminine. Most of the time, I'm okay with that. More than okay with that, actually. Sexy is not an adjective to which, in my saner moods, I aspire. Nevertheless, spending nine days last Christmas in the midst of a nation of pouty-lipped goddesses was enough to unearth every insecurity about my own beauty and femininity that I have. Every morning I walked out of my hotel thinking I looked my lovely best, and every night I returned to my room feeling like the dumpy, schlumpy, ugly step-sister.

"No wonder you're still single," the bad angel who apparently decided to go on pilgrimage with me kept whispering. "Look at them. Look at you. They're more feminine than you'll ever be."

In case you didn't already know this, bad angels lie.

Once sanity returned (and there was an ocean between me and women with thighs the size of toothpicks), I remembered that. I also remembered that all those impossibly thin, beautiful, and sexy Roman women aren't real. That is, the femininity they exude isn't real. Just like supermodels on a catwalk and centerfolds in *Playboy*, the sexually aggressive femininity that surrounded me in Rome is something of a sham—a cultural caricature of womanhood, an exaggerated grotesque of authentic femininity.

Which begs the question: What is "authentic femininity"?

The short answer is, "Two of the most charged words in the English language."

Utter them in a women's studies classroom, and you'll spark the equivalent of a barroom brawl. Utter them in a boardroom, and you'll be met with confused or bemused stares. Utter them in front of a mirror and you'll likely find yourself drowning in waves of insecurity and anxiety.

Rage. Denial. Self-doubt. All generated by two little words. Or rather, by people's misconceptions of two little words. In our culture, those misconceptions are legion. All too often, like those Roman beauties, they trap us and confuse us, leaving many of us with the distinct impression that no matter how hard we try, we can never measure up.

A Catholic Conundrum

This is true for women in general, but it's particularly true for single Catholic women, struggling with our single status and longing to be chosen.

Like other women in the culture, we hear the same problematic voices that equate femininity with all that's slinky, sexy, and hot. We also hear the voices that Catholic women hear, voices that sing the praises of motherhood and marriage while waxing poetic about the beauty of birth and new life. Then, there are the voices inside our own heads, the voices that accuse us of being betwixt and between those two ideals, of being neither goddess nor mother, neither desired nor beloved, and therefore not a real woman, not truly feminine, at all.

Over time, that cacophony of voices can start to operate like Chinese water torture, drip by drip driving us mad. It can corrode how we see ourselves. It can lead us to give in to the culture or give up on our heart's desires. It can make us bitter, angry, hard. It also can trigger some mighty destructive behaviors—promiscuity, eating disorders, self-mutilation.

That's why it's so important that we learn to discern truth from lies in all the chatter about femininity. If we want to move forward in our journey to a spouse and to God, as well as not drive ourselves crazy trying to measure up to some over-sexed, under-sexed, or completely idealized conception of womanhood, we need to shake off whatever bad ideas about femininity we've bought into over the years. We also need to pursue authentic femininity. We need to pursue being the women God calls us to be. In that, not with a husband and babies, is where true peace lies.

So, how do we begin that pursuit?

By separating the wheat from the chaff.

The Myths

First, the chaff.

No matter what *Vogue* or *Glamour* tells you, authentic femininity is not about your shape or your size. It has nothing to do with how closely you resemble the girl in the Pantene commercial or the bikini clad babe on the Budweiser billboard. It doesn't require or even recommend trying to conform yourself to the culture's standards of what beauty is. Slinky, sexy, and hot, it's most definitely not.

On the other hand, authentic femininity also doesn't necessitate following the advice of the crank who sits in the second pew at Mass every Sunday. At its core, the feminine genius cannot be boiled down to long hair, long skirts, and chapel veils. It is not the exclusive purview of homeschooling mothers of six (God bless their weary souls), nor does it require you to abandon your dreams of traveling the world, curing the sick, or opening your own small business.

Likewise, authentic femininity is not slang for "the repression of women." It doesn't entail a reversion to the days when women were supposed to be silly, simpering, and given to occasional fits of fainting. It's not about convincing intelligent women to mask their minds or opinions.

It's not about quelling your spirit or destroying your strength. It is not about becoming a plasticized version of St. Thérèse.

In his *Letter to Women*, Blessed John Paul II roundly dismissed those misconceptions in one swipe. Writing of women's great achievements in both public and private, he lamented: "Yet how many women have been and continue to be valued more for their physical appearance than for their skill, their professionalism, their intellectual abilities, their deep sensitivity; in a word, the very dignity of their being!"[1]

In sum, authentic femininity isn't about our looks, our reproductive output, or our resemblance to hagiographical accounts of Victorian children's saints. So, what is it about?

It's about being ourselves, our real and best selves, the women God made us to be. It's about reading the writing on our feminine souls—writing engraved there from the moment God formed us in our mothers' wombs—then living what that writing proclaims.

And the writing is there. Genesis 1 tells us as much.

The Anthropology

In Genesis, we learn that God made us in his image (Gen. 1:27). Obviously, that doesn't mean he gave us his eyes or his nose. It means he gave us his spirit, his life. He breathed it into us at the dawn of creation. As such, each and every human has the capacity to make visible some truth about the invisible God. In our ability to love, reason, create, and give, we resemble our Father, a God who is Love, who is Reason, who is the Creator, and who is Self-Gift.

God, however, didn't just make us in his image. He also made us male and female. He created two distinct ways of being human and imaging him. Today, some people like to reduce those two ways of being human to the level of biology—X chromosomes and Y chromosomes, male sex organs and female sex organs, that sort of thing. But that's not how it works.

As Catholics we know that "the body expresses the person."[2] In other words, our bodies reveal something about who we are. They make

---

1 John Paul II, *Letter to Women*, June 29, 1995, no 3. Available at http://www.vatican.va/holy_father/john_paul_ii/letters/documents/hf_jp-ii_let_29061995_women_en.html.

2 John Paul II, *Man And Woman He Created Them*, translated by Michael Waldstein (Pauline: 2006). See audiences for November 31, 1979; November 14, 1979; January 9, 1980; May 28, 1980.

visible the invisible truths of our inner lives, and they make visible the invisible differences between men and women. They embody and attest to those differences. They're not the extent of them. So, just as there are male and female bodies, there also are masculine souls and feminine souls, each corresponding to a masculine or feminine body, and each, in its own way, revealing something unique about God.

That's why when we talk about pursuing authentic femininity we're not talking about denying our true selves and conforming to someone else's idea of what women should be. Rather, we're talking about discovering our true selves, and becoming more the women God made us to be. We're also talking about imaging God as only women can.

That's not oppression. That's freedom.

From the Church

"The moral and spiritual strength of a woman is joined to her awareness that God *entrusts the human being to her in a special way*. Of course, God entrusts every human being to each and every other human being. But this entrusting concerns women in a special way— precisely by reason of their femininity—and this in a particular way determines their vocation . . . .

"*A woman is strong because of her awareness of this entrusting*, strong because of the fact that God 'entrusts the human being to her,' always and in every way, even in the situations of social discrimination in which she may find herself. This awareness and this fundamental vocation speak to women of the dignity which they receive from God himself, and this makes them 'strong' and strengthens their vocation."
—Blessed John Paul II, *Mulieris Dignatatem*, no. 30

The Genius

As for what exactly constitutes authentic femininity, well, there are reams of paper devoted to expounding on that. But the general consensus from the best of those reams is that there are at least three essential truths to which women, in body and soul, are called to witness.

First, women witness to the extent of God's love, to the pursuit he's on for each and every human soul.

God designed women, in both form and function, to be desired, pursued, and embraced. He designed us to attract, to fascinate, to elicit the same gasp of astonished wonder that Eve elicited from Adam in the Garden. And he didn't make us that way simply to ensure that humans would remain fruitful and multiply. He made us that way so that in our beauty, in men's desire for us, we would reveal how compelling the human soul is to God.

For reasons known only to him, God loves all his wayward and somewhat wacky creations with an unquenchable love. He desires each and every soul with an eternal desire. So he pursues. And when a soul surrenders to him, he draws that soul into an embrace that is always life giving. That embrace is the font of eternal life.

That's the first truth to which women are called to bear witness: Men and women are the desired and beloved of God.

The second is this: All is gift. All is grace.

You and I, whether we know it or not, are walking, breathing, talking, laughing signs of man's total and utter dependence on God. We can't help it. It's how we're built. Receptivity is, in many ways, the *sine qua non* of being feminine. God made us in such a way that we can receive our husband's body into our own body. He also made us in such a way that we can receive the gift of new life, a child, into our womb. Our body was designed to receive, and, as such, to show the world that we are all receivers. That nothing we have is our own. That life, grace, beauty, joy all flow into us from Another. And to that, faith, trust, and hope are the only possible responses.

The receptivity of our bodies, however, is supposed to be matched by the receptivity of our souls. We aren't just called to receive life, but to nourish and nurture it. In that, centuries of saints, writers, and philosophers insist, lies not only the third essential truth to which women are called to bear witness, but *the* essential truth, the true feminine genius.

We see that genius at work in those who have the gift for always making others feel welcome, cared for, and important, for bringing people into their homes, their world, and loving them as they most need to be loved. We see it too in those who give themselves in service to others—in the home, the workplace, the Church, and the community. All these women are able to do that because of a heart that's captured by the little and the least, ears that hear what the other has to say, and eyes that see the particular beauty of each individual. They're able to do that because they have a mother's soul.

And so do we all. At our core, that's who women are. That's what we're called to be, always in spirit, sometimes in body.

If you want to boil authentic femininity down to one word, "mother" is it. A mother is one who has been desired and beloved. She has received life into herself. And she nourishes and nurtures what she's received. That life might be the physical life of her children, born through union with her husband. Or it might be the spiritual life of the souls that surround her, spiritual life born of her fruitful union with her Creator to whom she is always beloved. Either way, the principle is the same. The genius is the same. And like all good things, it comes from God.

Women image a God who knows the number of hairs on his children's heads, who never breaks a bruised reed or snuffs a smoldering wick (Lk. 12:7, Is. 42:3). We reveal One who fed his people with manna in the desert and feeds his people now with his own body and blood in the Mass. We also reveal One who made a beautiful home for his children in creation and an even more beautiful home for them in his Church. That same God is a God who patiently and persistently calls all his children to himself and who holds the poor, suffering, and forgotten ever close to his heart. He never gives up. He never lets go. He is faithful to the end.

That's the image of God women bear in their souls. That's the image we're called to embody in the world. It has nothing to do with whether we're married or single, fertile or infertile, brunettes or redheads. Nor is it about what we do or don't do for a living. It's about *how* we do everything we do. It's about how we live in relation to God and how we live in relation to others. It's about being beautiful, receptive, and nurturing—always in spirit, sometimes in body—every day in every situation. The more we become capable of doing that, the more feminine we become.

The Feminine Genius on the Silver Screen:

Sometimes Hollywood actually does get it right. If you want to see the feminine genius in action, check out these authentically feminine characters on screen.

QUEEN MARY
(portrayed by Helena Bonham Carter) in *The King's Speech* (2010).

SISTER MARY BENEDICT
(portrayed by Ingrid Bergman) in *The Bells of St. Mary's* (1945).

BABETTE
(portrayed by Stéphane Audran) in *Babette's Feast* (1987).

MAE BRADDOCK
(portrayed by Renee Zelwegger) in *Cinderella Man* (2005).

ANNE ELLIOT
(portrayed by Amanda Root) in *Persuasion* (1995).

ELINOR DASHWOOD
(portrayed by Emma Thomason) in *Sense and Sensibility* (1995).

The Lesson Plan

But how do we become capable of doing that? How do we pursue the feminine genius?

It's one thing to say authentic femininity is all about being beautiful, receptive, and nurturing. It's another to actually be beautiful, receptive, and nurturing. Especially when the culture, our education, and sometimes even our own mothers tell us otherwise.

Since the days of grammar school, a good lot of us have been programmed to be anything but beautiful, receptive, and nurturing. We've been pushed to compete and compete hard. We've been told to put up emotional walls to protect ourselves. We've been encouraged to be controlling and aggressive—emotionally, professionally, sexually.

That pushing and encouraging has, at times, been explicit. It's come from the media, from TV shows, movies, and *Seventeen* magazine. It's also come from teachers, coaches, bosses, and parents. Other times, the encouragement has come by way of circumstance. Divorce, abuse, abandonment, and rejection all do their bit to quell the feminine genius.

Regardless, much of what should come naturally to us, what should be instinctive, no longer is. So we find ourselves, in this pursuit of femininity, needing to undo years of cultural programming.

That's not easy. There is no 12-step program to help us. But there is grace. There is prayer. And there are lessons to learn.

Lesson 1: Learn to Receive

This is where the happy, holy, sane train begins. Remember, "*sine qua non.*"

"Receive what?" you may ask. After all, no babies are in the offing just yet. But there's lots besides new life a woman needs to learn to receive. Such as . . .

Help: When you need it, ask, and when it's offered, take it. Also, love: Let people do nice things for you. Likewise, learn to receive counsel and correction: Someone always knows more than you. Learn to receive a compliment: With a smile and a "thank you." Learn to receive a man's attention: Let yourself be pursued. Learn how to receive others into your life and heart: Be vulnerable. Learn to receive a guest: Practice being welcoming and hospitable. Learn to receive knowledge: Read, study, and seek wisdom about man, the world, and God. Learn to receive the grace God longs to give you through his Word, through the sacraments, and through the writings of his saints: Go to him, daily.

And maybe start there. That will make receiving everything else a whole lot easier.

Lesson 2: Learn to Listen

There's no real receiving or nurturing without listening, so open up those ears. Listen to God. Listen to others. Hear what they have to say. Hear what they don't say. Listen to what they're passionate about, what they love, what they hate, what they struggle with, what they believe and don't believe. Listen to their heart, what moves them and motivates them. Listen as they reveal who they are. And while you do, practice being quiet. Work on not forming your own thoughts while the person speaking to you is still articulating theirs.

Lesson 3: Learn to Look and Act

What's true for the ears is true for the eyes. There's no loving without looking, so look. Look into people's eyes when they speak to you. Look into their hearts when they reveal them to you. Look for needs and wants. Look for gifts and talents. Look for the unique ways the people before you image God.

Look also around you. Who is alone? Who is neglected? Who is in need of company, a smile, or a cup of coffee on a snowy afternoon? Who needs your time and attention? Look for them and look away from yourself.

Then, finally, act on what you see. Respond rightly. Put yourself out there for others. Follow Mary's lead at Cana. Don't let legitimate needs go unmet. Make like Esther in Persia and speak out against injustice. Pull a Rahab and aid those fighting for a righteous cause. Whatever you do, don't let wounds go uncared for. Don't let anyone walk away from you feeling unloved, unappreciated, and unimportant. Be an advocate for all who need one.

Your Guide

If you're looking to cultivate authentic femininity, there's no surer guide than the Blessed Mother. As John Paul II wrote in his *Letter to Women*, "The Church sees in Mary the highest expression of the 'feminine genius.'"

So go to her in difficulties great and small. Talk to her. Look upon her in works of art. Study her. Say her Rosary daily.

Like all good mothers, Mary will always come to your assistance. But unlike your own mother, when you mess up, she'll never say, "I told you so."

Lesson 4: Learn to Submit

Not to your controlling ex-boyfriend, but to God, to truth, to what is right and good. Yield your mind to the Holy Spirit so he can form it according to truth. Yield your plans to his in every day, hour, and moment. Yield your need for understanding in the face of sorrow and suffering. Stand before the mystery and accept that God's ways are not our ways.

Likewise, submit to the moral law and the Church's teachings. Go to Confession when you don't. Face every obstacle with "Not my will but thine" on your lips and in your heart. Give God permission to mold you and form you into the woman he made you to be. He only acts on you with your permission. Give it.

⁂

Lesson 5: Learn to Endure

Way back on Calvary, after the Apostles jumped ship, the women were still there, standing by Christ's side. And while Peter and company hid in shuttered rooms, the women were braving Roman guards to visit Christ's tomb. That's because women endure. We are a faithful sex, a tenacious sex. So be tenacious. Learn to love longer and harder. Learn to hold on when all hope seems lost. Learn to wait, be patient, and suffer without needless complaint. Turn the other cheek. Never give up on anyone. Be the persistent widow. Nag God: He can take it.

⁂

Lesson 6: Learn Gentleness

If you don't want to break the bruised reed, learn to control your strength. Learn how and when to address conflicts. Don't raise but rather lower your voice when you're angry. Speak honestly, but in the right ways and at the right times. Learn when counsel is needed, and learn when it's just sympathy that's called for. Temper just criticism with kindness. Temper complaints with appropriate words of affirmation. Temper your opinions with some consideration for others. Think not just about what you want to say, but also about how others will hear what you say. Basically, don't be a hammer. At least not a big one. And no matter how much you want to hit or throw things, don't. Go for a walk instead.

⁂

Lesson 7: Learn to Appreciate and Cultivate Beauty

Remember, we're the beautiful sex—the sex that reflects the beauty of God, as well as his penchant for creating beautiful things for his children to enjoy. So follow suit. Learn to paint. Learn to sew. Learn to make pottery. Learn how to set a beautiful table, arrange your furniture, and hang pictures. Study the difference between Bach and Beethoven. Go to a museum and look upon the handiwork of the Pre-Raphaelites. Plant tulip bulbs. Heck, just clean out your closet.

Also thank God every morning for all the beautiful things with which he's surrounded you. Appreciate his handiwork. Thank him for the big, grand beauties—the sun, the moon, the stars—plus the much more prosaic bits of beauty which are even more plentiful—shiny steel pots, icy blue cashmere sweaters, the cute guy at the coffee shop. You get the picture. The more you thank God for beauty, the more beauty you'll see. Guaranteed.

Lesson 8: Learn Modesty

Again, we're the beautiful sex. But it's God's beauty we ultimately want people to gaze upon, so don't be a distraction from that. Don't be an object. Be a subject, with value, dignity, and mystery. Learn to dress fashionably and beautifully without dressing suggestively. Keep those hemlines around the knee or below and stock up on camisoles. Save the yoga pants for when you're actually doing yoga. Cover up those shoulders in church. Learn how to sit in a skirt (legs together, ankles crossed) and how to draw attention to your face and eyes, not your chest (Say yes to the mascara, no to the plunging neckline). While you're at it, learn what talk is and isn't appropriate in mixed company. And know how to gently arch an eyebrow when someone else forgets.

Lesson 9: Learn What Real Beauty Is

I keep saying it. God made you to be beautiful. Not to be a supermodel, but beautiful, lovely. Learn what lovely means. Learn that the source of your beauty is not your clothing size, but rather the fact that you were created by God, who loves you and desires to be with you. Know that from your relationship with him flows all that makes you beautiful in his eyes—a prayerful soul, a humble spirit, a selfless heart.

Learn also one of the implications of John Paul II's words, "The body expresses the person." That is, whatever is on the inside eventually shows up on the outside. No matter what the magazines say, in the long run, the surest way to make yourself unattractive to both God and good men is to have a soul infested by vanity, immodesty, vulgarity, and promiscuity. Conversely, a beautiful spirit will always make itself known through a smile, a laugh, a body that moves with grace, or a voice that speaks with intelligence. All those things and a thousand more factor in to how attractive people think you are. Beauty is more than the sum of one's parts.

The Catholic Single Girl's Closet

There are few hard-and-fast rules for authentically feminine dress. Mostly it's about what's modest, flattering, and "you." But "few" is not the same as "none."

The Essentials . . . If you have 'em, great. If not, start shopping.
Lots of camisoles, cardigans, and leggings (to make much that's not wearable, wearable), a skirt that swings and swishes, a pencil skirt (if you can carry it off), a couple great scarves, two pairs of tall boots—one brown, one black (to make those skirts both feasible and fashionable in the winter), ballet flats, one fabulous cocktail dress, a comfortable and flattering (i.e., not skin tight) pair of jeans.

The Banned List . . . What needs to go and stay gone.
Mini-skirts, short shorts, tube tops, jeggings, pants or skirts with lettering across the backside, halter tops with plunging necklines, uber-high heels (no, no, a thousand times no), leather pants or skirts, denim or corduroy jumpers, strapless anything (unless paired with a shawl or cardigan), body glitter.

Lesson 10: Learn to Look Lovely

One more time: The body expresses the person. So let the beauty you're striving for on the inside be reflected on the outside. Learn to look lovely. Learn to be graceful, put together, healthy, and confident, eschewing both immodesty and slovenliness. Tend to the face and body with which God blessed you. Invest in sunscreen, quality soap, and creams that protect, rather than damage, your skin. Exercise regularly and eat right, not to control the shape of your body, but to care for it, to honor it. Never forget, it's a temple. Grow your hair out if it looks best long. If it looks better short, then chop chop. Wear a *little* makeup. Learn firsthand that comfortable and fashionable are not mutually exclusive realities. Dress in clothes that flatter and fit. Buy A-line skirts. Skip the jeggings. Dig that iron out of your closet. Above all, smile.

From the 'Edith Stein Says It Better' File

"The soul of a woman must therefore be *expansive* and open to all human beings; it must be *quiet* so that no small weak flame will be extinguished by stormy winds; *warm* so as not to benumb fragile buds; *clear* so that no vermin will settle in dark corners and recesses; *self-contained* so that no invasions from without can peril the inner life; *empty of itself*, in order that extraneous life may have room in it; finally, *mistress of itself* and also of its body, so that the entire person is readily at the disposal of every call."

—St. Edith Stein,
"Fundamental Principles of Women's Education," *Woman*

That, in a nutshell, is how you cultivate authentic femininity. Or at least it's a start. I'd bet my house there are lessons to learn that I haven't discovered yet, just as I'd bet the same there are lessons on that list that you've already mastered far better than I (cough…cough…gentleness…cough…cough). Nevertheless, the list is something to get you started or keep you going in your pursuit of the feminine genius.

What it shouldn't do, however, is confuse you about your final destination. The lessons every woman needs to master may be the same. But the end products of those lessons won't be. Authentic femininity doesn't work that way.

You see, God didn't just create two versions of being human, male and female. He created billions. Every soul is an unrepeatable work of wonder. Accordingly, how each of us lives out our orientation to motherhood, how we receive, how we listen, how we cultivate beauty and care for others, will be different from how every other woman does those things.

God made some of us to love knitting by a fireside in long, flowing skirts and he made others to love hiking in the Cascades in boots and jeans. He made some of us to love both. That's great. That's how it's supposed to be. That's what makes life interesting and surprising. And again, the goal of holiness is never to become a clone of St. Thérèse, St. Clare, or the Virgin

Mary. The goal is to become you, a beautiful, one-of-a-kind daughter of God. Voices that tell you otherwise should be roundly dismissed.

There's also another voice that needs to be roundly dismissed. That's the voice inside our own heads, which can convince us that this whole pursuing authentic femininity thing is about our search for a husband, that if only we learn to listen a little better or become a smidge more gentle our wedding day will finally dawn.

That might be the case. But it also might not be. There are plenty of lovely, feminine women walking around unmarried in this world, just as there are plenty of women who don't give a fig about femininity sporting a diamond ring on their left hand.

No, the pursuit of authentic femininity isn't something we do because we're pursuing a husband. It's not a mercenary undertaking, and if we think of it that way, we'll never attain it. Rather, the pursuit of authentic femininity is something we do because we're pursuing happiness and holiness. That, both now and long after the husband arrives, is what the business of our life is all about.

Of course, there is still that matter of looking for a husband. But that involves something far more difficult than pursuing authentic femininity. It involves (cue horror-flick scream in background) . . . Dating.

Ask the
Single Girl

Dear Single Girl,

After years of renting, I feel like I'm throwing cash down the drain. I'm toying with the idea of buying, but have been told that will scare off a husband. Any thoughts on single women owning homes?

—Renting in Raleigh

Dear Renting,

Oh, do I have thoughts. Let's set aside the husband quandary for a minute, however, and deal with the more practical things you need to consider.

First, home ownership is expensive. In the short term, it's even more expensive than renting. That's because things break. Furnaces, dishwashers, toilets, windows, air conditioners, front doors and backdoors, bathroom faucets, attic fans, stair rails—you name it, it breaks. And you're responsible for the cost of repairs. Over time, those costs may not add up to the cost of renting, but they still put a strain on your pocketbook. So if you buy, be prepared for those expenses.

Home ownership can also be exhausting. Dealing with all those things that break (and the repairmen who come to fix them) can test the patience of a saint. Then there are the random duties built into home ownership: changing air filters, waterproofing your deck, mowing your lawn, shoveling the snow. Unless you're looking to buy a condo, say goodbye to lazy Saturday afternoons. Big decisions about your house, such as whether or not to remodel your kitchen, can also be hard to make alone. Other people can give you advice, but unlike a spouse, they're not invested in your ultimate decision, and having to make one big financial decision after another all by yourself can leave you feeling more alone than ever.

These aren't, however, insurmountable obstacles. If you have loads of cash, they're quite minor. If you have handy brothers or male friends living close by (or if you're willing to acquire some plumbing skills yourself), they're likewise manageable. What's not as manageable, however, is the real estate market. When it's bad, your dream home can become a millstone around your neck, keeping you in one place when you desperately want to be in another. If that other place is where a new job is, that's bad. If it's where your fiancée is, that's even worse.

That being said, I happen to be the proud owner of a one hundred-year-old money pit that I absolutely adore. It's beautiful, gracious, and all I ever wanted my house to be. Which it better be. Over the past six years, I've spent thousands of hours and tens of thousands of dollars making it that way.

I don't regret my decision. For me it's been a good one, and if I had to do it over, I would make the same choice. That's partly because I live in a city where "nice rentals" don't exist. I also have a habitual desire (some would say "compulsion") to strip wood, replaster walls, and paint everything that doesn't move. Besides, I like having something beautiful that's mine—something that I'll either sell (and walk away with a handsome down payment for another home) or that I'll own outright, with no rent to pay and no landlord to thwart my painting demons.

Which brings me to that husband question. I'm not sure where you're getting your information, but the guys I know and respect (married and unmarried) think it's cool that I can reglaze windows and mud a wall. They also appreciate my ability to create a beautiful, warm, welcoming home where they get to hang out. From what they tell me, those are pluses in the desirability equation, not minuses, as is the nest egg I'll have if I ever sell this place. And honestly, I have no interest in being with a guy who thinks otherwise. I don't want to marry someone who finds my ability to make good life decisions intimidating. Do you?

Getting back to the bigger picture, there is both a serious cost and a serious value to homeownership. Whether the value is worth the cost to you isn't something I can answer. All I can advise is to make sure you're not letting HGTV's charming picture of home ownership or some naysayer's prediction of house-induced spinsterhood cloud your vision. Be realistic. Know the cost, know yourself, and know your ability to pay that cost. Then act accordingly.

And if you're ever in the market for a depreciating piece of Steubenville real estate, give me a call.

Everything the Catholic Single Girl
Needs to Know About . . .

The Dos and Don'ts of Dating

I admit it. There's something both ironic and a bit unseemly about a single woman giving advice on dating. Even in my own head a snarky little voice keeps repeating, "Cause it's worked out so well for you, hasn't it?"

Nevertheless, the advice must be given. First, because dating (or some version thereof) is the only way we're going to get out of this single existence of ours. Second and most importantly, because bad dating behaviors are one of the surest ways to mess with our sanity. They either lead us into bad relationships, which God forbid could end in bad marriages, or they leave us with wounds and regrets that can haunt us for years after a relationship ends.

Besides, after having done a brief survey of the books and articles about dating currently on the market, I have concluded that if child brides and celibate priests can give advice on dating, so can unmarried women. The truth is, there are few people with more dating experience than single people in their thirties and forties. It just, unfortunately, hasn't been experience gained with the right person. Ours is a wisdom born more from failure than success, but it is, nevertheless, wisdom, and the more I've learned to heed my own advice, the easier and less traumatizing this whole dating thing has become.

Please note, however: I said "easier," not "easy." Also, "less traumatizing," not "a walk through a park on a sunny day."

Once upon a time, in my teens and twenties, I thought both roller coaster rides and dating were about equally fun. After all, they weren't that different. Both came with soaring highs and plummeting lows. Both were all chills, thrills, and butterflies. But at thirty-five, I find I have little appetite for soaring highs or plummeting lows. Butterflies have lost their thrill, and the memory of one too many chills quells my thirst for more. Basically, roller coaster rides now scare me and dating exhausts me.

Accordingly, these days I'm wont to say that I don't want to date at all anymore; I just want to get married. Based upon my conversations with other women from their mid-twenties on up, this dating weariness is pretty typical. The glow is gone. We're tired of doing as adults what we did as teenagers. We're ready to move on and move on fast.

But how exactly do we think we're going to do that without dating? It's a bit of a Catch 22, isn't it? We're tired of one thing and desiring another. But in order to get what we desire we need to do exactly that which tires us so.

Or do we?

Faceoff: Courtship vs. Dating

There is, some would say, another way of attaining what we desire: Courtship.

For the uninitiated, courtship is a way of journeying to "I do" that is structured very differently from modern dating. Although there are different models of courtship, in general it involves a man slowly getting to know a woman in a non-romantic, community setting over a period of time in order to discern whether or not she is potential spouse material (She is, of course, discerning the same). If the verdict of both parties is yes, the guy requests permission from the girl's parents to "court." Once courting begins, marriage is always explicitly on the table. Couples can spend more time alone together, but the relationship still takes place primarily in the context of community and family life. The courting phase is also, at least compared to modern dating, brief, lasting anywhere from a few months to a year or two, no more. Short engagements are also typical.

The thinking of courtship proponents is that courtship circumvents many of the downsides of dating. In other words, the slow pace, intentional focus on marriage, group settings, shorter periods of romantic involvement, and participation of the family are supposed to act as a check against the fast-paced, hormone-driven, exclusivity of serial dating that often clouds our judgment, puts us in situations not exactly conducive to keeping our virtue, and rapidly leads us from one broken heart to another.

In theory, the pro-courtship folks are mostly right. There are all sorts of advantages to slow-moving, friendship-driven, community-based relationships, not the least of which is a proven track record of longer, more lasting marriages. Courtship, after all, is how the human race married itself off for most of its existence, right up until the modern age.

But, as great as no awkward first dates, no pressure to get too physical too fast, and no sorting through online profiles via Catholic Match sounds, is traditional courtship actually feasible? In a world where dating is almost as habitual as breathing, can a slower, more deliberate, and prayerful method of mating work? Can we get what we say we want: marriage without dating?

The answer, I think, is "occasionally" and "to an extent."

For young people still in college—where lots of non-romantic group activity happens naturally—and for those who live close to parents who are capable of and willing to do what courtship requires of them, the traditional courtship model (or some variation thereof) can, and often does, work great.

For the rest of us, however, it's a bit trickier. Too many of us live and work far from our parents, parents who may not be as faithful or traditional as we are and who would laugh at the mere idea of them selecting our spouse. And really, how many of us want to turn over that responsibility to our parents? Personally, I love my mom loads, but I won't let her pick out clothes for me, let alone the man with whom I'm going to spend the rest of my life.

Then, there's the little problem that courtship requires two willing parties who've completely bought into this alternative mode of dating.

You may be one, but there's no guarantee the cute guy from church will be the other. Also as we've already established, healthy, sane, faithful men are in rather short supply these days. When we find one, few of us—dating weary though we may be—are of a mind to hit the pause button on any blossoming romance. Likewise, if the guy is free of any commitment issues, mommy issues, and discernment issues, he's even less of a mind to "just be friends" for indefinite amounts of time.

Clearly, for a whole lot of us, traditional courtship isn't realistic. But neither is the way the post-modern culture does dating. Early and intense romantic involvement, dating as a recreational activity and not as a means of intentionally discerning marriage, culturally sanctioned sex by the third date, and shacking up as soon as things get "serious"—all with a steady succession of romantic partners—are not activities in which nice Catholic girls can partake. Not if happy, holy Catholic marriages and happy holy Catholic lives are what we're after.

Remember, that type of dating is a big part of the reason why you and I are in the boat we're in. It's also a big part of the reason why 25 percent of all marriages end in divorce within the first five years.[1] And yes, I understand, not all "dating" ends in cohabitation. You can "date" without violating any moral norms (although that's much more of a feat than it used to be). What you can't do, however, is hop from boyfriend to boyfriend, giving your heart again and again, and having the gift rejected (or taking it back yourself) again and again, without incurring some pretty nasty wounds. Long-term serial dating makes us less able and less willing to give ourselves to the right person. It also makes it more likely that we'll take the gift back once we give it. It conditions us to relational patterns that are anything but "for as long as we both shall live."

So, what are good Catholic girls like us to do?

---

1 2007 CARA report, "Marriage in the Catholics Church: A Survey of U.S. Catholics." Available at www.cara.georgetown.edu.

Code Red

 It's uncontestable: Pickin's are slim. But guys who fall in the following categories should flag a Code Red warning in your mind. In other words, run. Run fast.

Discerning Men: If he's discerning there's the double risk of you getting your heart broken when he decides he needs to get himself to seminary or of him abandoning the priestly vocation to which God is calling him. Let him discern and if what he discerns is you, he'll come calling.

Dating Men: If he's dating someone else and makes a move on you before breaking off the first relationship, he's not to be trusted. Plain and simple.

Divorced Men: All marriages are presumed valid until proven otherwise, so if there's no annulment, in the eyes of the Church this guy is still married. And dating married men is wrong. Confessable wrong. You can be friends. You can hang out in groups. But you can't do anything that, if he were still living with his wife, would give her just cause for complaint. If the man obtains an annulment, that's a different matter, but until then, he's off limits.

Married Men: I'm not even going to explain this one.

First, pray for a miracle . . . regularly.

Second, we need to find some middle ground, a mode of dating that incorporates some of the best aspects of courtship—chastity, friendship, prayer, and slow, intentional, marriage-oriented discernment—and avoids the worst habits of contemporary dating—getting serious, exclusive, and intimate too fast, dating purely for entertainment, companionship, affirmation, or affection, and moving through a string of romantic partners in steady succession.

I wish I could give you a cut-and-dried formula for doing that. But I can't. Every person and every relationship is different. Even if you think you know exactly the best way to go about it, there's still going to be another person with ideas of his own involved. Finding the right balance between both of your preferences (and doing so without harming either of your souls) is a trick you'll have to manage mostly on your own.

But only mostly.

Like always, there are some basic rules that can help: tried and true dos and don'ts of looking for a mate that can save both parties a whole lot of heartache and make the process of discerning a spouse that much easier.

Before I launch into my "sage-like" list of dos and don'ts, however, let me remind you of two things.

First, to almost every (*but not every*) rule, there is an exception.

Second, odds are, you aren't the exception.

How Long, Oh Lord?

Dating is not like baking a cake. You can't put it on a timer. Six months, twelve months, sixty-eight months—no one timeframe is right for how fast all relationships should develop. Depending on the people, the issues, and the situation each is in, the timing itself will be different.

With that in mind, long engagements are generally dangerous. They leave both parties open to more temptations against chastity. The same goes for prolonged dating relationships, which come with the same temptations, plus entangle people in long-term relationships that may be going nowhere. On the other hand, not knowing the person long enough, and not having a solid friendship on which you can build a marriage, is equally dangerous. Whirlwind courtships and engagements pose as much if not more of a risk than lengthy ones. Unless one of you is dying, it's near impossible to justify marrying someone you've known less than a year. It won't hurt you to wait a bit and will probably help.

In short, each couple has to be aware of the inherent dangers in moving too fast or to slow, and with the counsel of friends and spiritual advisors, find the timeframe that's right for them.

Starting Principles

Do Know What You Want

By this I don't mean "Six feet tall, athletic, goes to daily Mass, likes Indian food, and reads C.S. Lewis." I'm not talking about lists. Lists are a bad idea. We're all much more than the sum of our parts, and trying to enumerate the parts for which we're searching can lead us in the exact opposite direction from where we actually want (and need) to be. No, what I'm talking about is the big picture, what we ultimately want (or should want) out of our interactions with the opposite sex.

Not to sound trite, but we need to remember, men are people too. They do not exist simply to make us feel pretty and desirable, pay for dinner and shows, or to put a diamond ring on our finger.

But sometimes we single girls can forget that. We approach every interaction with every remotely eligible man with marriage in mind. Or we approach every interaction with men in general as an opportunity to get what we want from them: attention, affection, affirmation. Both approaches are problematic. They tend to lead us quickly and frequently into the wrong kind of relationship with the wrong kind of guy. Also, whether we realize it or not, they reduce men to objects . . . which they aren't.

Guys have so much to offer us besides romance—friendship, wisdom, laughter—but in order to receive that, we have to see them first and foremost as brothers in Christ, as fellow travelers on the journey to holiness. We have to respect them for who they are, not for what they can give us or what we'd like them to be. When we do that, we create the space for friendship to grow. We lay the foundation for a real relationship based on mutual admiration, appreciation, and concern. That in itself is a good and noble thing. It's also the only foundation on which a lasting, healthy Christian marriage can be built. And that, not simply a ring or a few compliments, is what we ultimately want.

Do Be Picky

Yes, this flies in the face of Aunt Muriel's remedy for ending your singlehood. But the thing is, I don't know a single Catholic woman who is too picky. No one I know is looking for Mr. Perfect. We're looking for Mr. Right. And we fully expect him to come with his share of flaws.

On the other hand, I do know an awful lot of women who should have been *more* picky, who should have valued themselves more than they did and exercised much greater caution in the selection process.

Here's the deal. Marriage is hard. Really, really hard. It's harder today than ever before. People are more messed up. Traditional support structures have all but disappeared. And even the marriages of some seemingly strong and faithful Catholics are ending in divorce. For a marriage to succeed, both partners have to be mature, highly functioning adults with a strong sense of responsibility and fidelity. They not only have to know right from wrong, they also have to be capable of choosing the right over the wrong. Unfortunately, men who fit that bill are a heck of a lot rarer than your Aunt Muriel thinks.

Don't Be Unrealistic

I know, you're not looking for Mr. Perfect, just Mr. Right. But make sure your picture of Mr. Right is just that, *your* picture of Mr. Right, not Hollywood's. You know the guys you see on the silver screen, the ones who say and do the most beautiful things, who are always tender, sensitive, and emotionally present to the heroine in need? Well, those are fictional characters written mostly by women and gay men. In real life, men aren't like matinee heroes. They're more like men. Which is a good thing. Men are splendid. But if you're expecting the matinee hero, you will be sorely disappointed. So, don't.

Expect instead that words of affirmation and consolation will not always drip sweetly and easily from your beloved's lips. Expect him to get frustrated when you repeat the same complaint about your mother more than once in the same conversation. Expect him to want to fix every problem you have and not want to keep talking through those problems once he's devised a solution. Expect him to make broad statements about general concepts without having any idea that you're taking every broad statement he makes personally. Expect him to want to order and categorize, in the most minute detail, at least one thing in the universe— his checkbook, his library, fifty years of Steelers stats. Expect him to be quiet when he's upset, angry and irritable when he's stressed, and oblivious to how much it hurts you when he talks about his ex-girlfriends.

At the same time, expect him to want to come to your rescue when your tire blows on the highway. Expect him to want to drive, pay for movie tickets, ask questions in public, and do all the other little things that he believes are involved in taking care of you. Expect him to delight in telling you every possible detail about the subjects or things he's most passionate about—philosophy, politics, his MacBook Pro—and expect him to expect you to be equally delighted by the knowledge he's imparting. Expect him to dig his heels in when you nag and blossom like a rose in June when you praise. Expect him to brag a little more than he ought in your presence and conceal mistakes he's made—not because he's deceptive but because he cares more about your approval than anyone else's: He doesn't just want your respect, he needs it. Lastly, expect him to struggle more than he lets on with chastity and his own attraction to you.

Basically expect him to be a man and not a woman. Know his thoughts are not your thoughts and his ways are not your ways. Rejoice in the differences, and recognize that anything but *would be* disappointing.

Don't Think You Have to Be Someone Other Than Who You Are
Inside every single woman's head is an evil voice. The voice may be her mother's. It may be some silly author she once read. It may be her own. Regardless, the first four words it utters are always the same: "You're not married because . . ."

What follows varies. You're not married because you're too fat. You're not married because you're too smart. You're not married because you're not smart enough . . . or because your hair isn't long . . . or because you don't wear skirts . . . or because you don't hide your opinions . . . or because you're too tall, too thin, too short, too fair, too dark.

The list is almost endless. It's also nonsense. Or mostly nonsense.

Perhaps you have some deep-seeded issue preventing you from committing to a man, getting close to a man, or even being nice to a man. That's a question to put to your best friends. As for the rest, well, think about the women you know who are married, the women from work, school, church, or the neighborhood. What are they like?

That's right. They're short and tall, thin and fat, brilliant and batty, opinionated and empty-headed, pious and impious, short-haired and long-haired, stunners and downright scary looking. Some wear pants. Some wear skirts. Some cook. Some burn water. Some are arch-normal. Others are the oddest ducks around. And you know what? Someone married them anyhow. They didn't change who they were in order to find a husband. They didn't force themselves to conform to someone's ideal of Catholic womanhood. They were the person God made them to be, and they found men who loved them that way. God willing, so will you.

On Missionary Dating

To date a non-Catholic or not date a non-Catholic? That is the question, isn't it? Unfortunately it's not a question with an easy answer. Dating, let alone marrying, a guy who doesn't share your core beliefs is an exercise fraught with danger. It can make chastity hard now and any number of things—remaining open to life, passing on the faith to your children, and simply staying together—heartbreakingly hard in the future.

Nevertheless, there are plenty of women out there who discerned they were called to date a Protestant or somewhat lapsed Catholic and that, as it turned out, became part of God's plan for bringing that man into (or back into) the Church. Sometimes missionary dating pays off. But sometimes it doesn't. And no matter what, it's never easy. It requires a great deal of honesty and a great many difficult discussions. It can also force you to feel as if compromising core beliefs and behaviors is the only way to make a relationship work. Only you can discern with a great deal of prayer if this is what God's calling you to do. And if you discern that it is, discern again, just to be sure.

That being said, it's one thing to date someone who is serious about his or her Christian faith. It's an entirely different thing to date someone who isn't serious about any faith. They will expect things of you that you cannot and must not give. And you will want things from them that they are not capable of giving. In this culture, in all but the rarest of circumstances, it's safe to say that non-Christians and seriously lapsed believers are off limits. Remember, marriage and romance aren't the ultimate ends you seek. What you're after is holiness, and your relationships in this life need to serve that end.

Don't Be Proud

Say yes to the set-up. I know, these are generally about as fun as finding the square root of the tiles on your kitchen floor. But every once in a while, it works. Accordingly, don't let your ego stop you from accepting help when it's offered. Likewise, don't let your pride prevent you from reminding friends that if they know any eligible young men it would be lovely if they sent them your way. Seriously, in the current marriage market, single gals need all available help.

Don't Pursue

This rule applies to the guys you haven't gone out with as well as the guys you have. The chase is not yours. It's his. And if he's interested and able, he will chase. He really will. So, don't ask him out. Wait for him to ask you. Don't call him up right after a date. Wait for him to call you. And for Pete's sake, don't hound him with emails. Just reply to his.

This doesn't mean you can't gently encourage a man to call or ask you out. But a smile and a show of genuine interest whenever he's talking will usually be sufficient. It also doesn't mean you can't invite a guy whom you've got your eye on to a party at your house or an evening out with your friends. Group outings are a great way to break the ice. That, however, is it. Anything more and you start to look both desperate and aggressive, neither of which are very attractive qualities in a woman and both of which, I'm afraid to say, are almost guaranteed to get you talked about amongst his friends.

Getting Started: The First Few Dates

Do Let Him Be the Guy

The first date is not the time to fly your feminist flag. Guys like being guys. They like showing off the training their mama gave them and proving that they're thoughtful, sensitive, and clever enough to give a woman a lovely night out. That is, they do if they're worth their salt. So let them. Let your date open the doors, help you with your coat, and pay for dinner. Let him plan the evening. If he asks for suggestions and you have some, feel free to share. Just don't try to control him or the date. Enjoy him and enjoy the fact that someone is trying to please you. Also, be grateful. Appreciate his efforts. Thank him, with words and a smile, for everything he does right, and, unless absolutely necessary, make no mention of what he does wrong.

Don't Reveal Too Much

The first few dates are the time to talk books, baseball, and politics. Not possible babies and past loves. It's when you discuss school and work, hobbies and roommates, travel experiences and favorite foods. Not sins and psychological disorders. The Church, faith, and the sacraments, funny stories from your childhood, and charming anecdotes about your family all can supply hours of conversational material. Which is to say, there's no need to resort to intimate revelations. In fact, there's a need not to. Revealing too much too fast puts you at risk of being misunderstood and undervalued. You need to know whom you're exposing your heart to before you expose it. A few emails or even a few dates aren't enough for that. So take it slow. Keep a little mystery about you. And guard your heart. In time, with the right person, you can take those defenses down.

Don't Start Planning the Wedding After the First Date
Or the third, or the twenty-third. In fact, don't start planning the wedding until you actually have a ring on your finger. No matter how great a guy seems at first, there's a lot you both need to know about each other before you commit yourself body and soul to him. So detach. Don't get too excited. Keep a spirit of cautious optimism about you, hoping things will only get better, but not expecting that you're on the fast track to David's Bridal. And when those expectations rise up in spite of your best efforts, just offer them to God. He'll know what to do with them.

Do Give Him A Chance
Okay, I'll be honest. I'm the queen of nixing it after the first date. Sometimes it's been for good reasons—the guy who mysteriously turned into an octopus as soon as the lights dimmed in the theatre. Other times it's been for *very* good reasons—one misguided soul dared confess a distaste for garlic. Nevertheless, I've learned over time not to be too hasty. Nerves, excitement, flashbacks of former flames, fear of rejection, the desire to make a good first impression—all these and more are reasons why first dates aren't the best indicator of whether or not someone is a real possibility for you. You say silly things. He says stupid things. Rarely does the date or the guy himself measure up to your expectations.

That's why you should do yourself (and him) a favor and take some of the pressure off. Go into the date resolved to not make up your mind right away. Expect to not be head over heels in love by the end of the night. Be prepared to give him a second chance. When you do, he just might surprise you.

Don't Waste His Time
Like I said, second chances are good. Necessary even. But most of the time, by the third date, enough chances have been had. You either know

you could possibly be serious about a person or you know that "just friends" is all you'll ever be. So make the call after date number three (or date number five if you want to be really generous). If you're not convinced by the end of that date that the guy has serious marriage potential, let him down kindly. Anything else is dating just to date, and that quickly turns into using—using another person to fill a hole in your life or heart, to feel better about yourself, or to avoid being alone. Whatever the reason, doing it is as bad for you as it is for him. It's not going to bring either of you lasting happiness, and it may get in the way of one or both of you meeting the person who is right for you.

Off and Running: The Relationship

Do Spend Lots of Time with His (and Your) Friends

His friends were there long before you. They may be there long after you. And no matter what, they're probably not going anywhere. That's why when he wants to plan a day or evening with you and his friends (or family), you need to be a yes-man. Get to know the people he loves. Try to understand why he loves them. Most importantly, observe who he is around them.

Generally you can learn more about a guy from one evening spent in the company of his friends then you can in a half-dozen romantic dinners. Alone with you, he's putting on his best self. In a group with his friends, he can't help but be his real self. You might like what you see or you might not. Either way, you score points with him for happily hanging out with his friends and you score points with his friends for not being the girl who gets in the way of his other relationships. That is, you score points if you're nice. So be nice.

What's true for him and his friends is true for you and yours. If you want him to know you, the real you, he needs to see you in your native habitat, doing the things you love with the people you love. Moreover, while his sparkling green eyes may hypnotize you, they're not going to hypnotize your friends. Which means they may see things you don't—warning signs, reasons for concern, or problematic habits of relating between you two. Your friends love you. They want the best for you. And they know you better than anyone. Give them the opportunity to form some opinions, and even if you don't like the opinions they form, do consider them. They're probably right.

* * * * * * * * * * * * * * * * *

Don't Abandon Your Girlfriends

Girlfriends are not nice extras in the game of life, expendable and disposable when Mr. Right comes along. You need these women. Desperately. They are the ones who will reassure you seven times seventy that you are not fat. They are the ones who will happily discuss clothes, relationships and your new living room wall color with you. They don't mind when you repeat yourself, they know just what to say when you're sad, and they understand how totally mind-altering female hormones can be. Again, you need these women. Your sanity and, by default, your boyfriend/future husband's sanity depends upon them. Don't neglect them. Don't stop calling and don't start cancelling plans with them as soon as a new man comes into your life. Always carve out time for them, and when you're with them, try to temper the talk about your new love. Remember, these women need you too. You're their sanity check and support system. If you can't be that, they'll go elsewhere. And there's no guarantee they'll come back.

* * * * * * * * * * * * * * * * *

Do Be Interested in What He's Interested In

Every guy has his passion. It may be computers. It may be NASCAR. It may be books. And no matter how much he loves you, that passion won't wane. He's not going to care about the Pirates box scores any less because you're in his life. So, unless that passion is something highly problematic (such as spending hours playing Grand Theft Auto) don't try to force him to give that passion up. Don't sulk when he turns on the game in the car. Don't pout when he goes off to Indianapolis for the weekend. Don't get angry when he says he wants to spend his Saturday morning reading instead of going out to breakfast with you. Even if you get your way in the short-term, you lose in the long term. He will resent you for coming between him and his first love.

It doesn't have to be a competition, however, between you and the Packers or you and Scott Hahn. If the guy you love loves this thing, there must be something lovable about it. Try to love it. Try to be interested. Try to share his passion.

Code Orange

Unlike the guys who flag a Code Red, you don't necessarily need to run helter-skelter at the first sign of a Code Orange. You just need to be careful. Sticking with one of these fellows requires a lot more prayer and discernment than sticking with your average Joe. And if you discern to proceed, proceed with *extreme* caution.

Super-Slow Movers. Beware men who, after more than a couple months of casual dating or hanging around, haven't made their intentions clear. Maybe they genuinely need more time. Maybe God really wants you to give them that time. It is possible. But it's unlikely. More likely is that they're either (a) not that interested in you, or (b) not that interested in committing to anyone just yet.

Super-Fast Movers. Equally beware men who after the second or third date pledge their undying love and propose marriage. These eager beavers may be the nicest of guys, and you may be the most amazing of women, but de facto marriage proposals after the third date tend to signal that the guy doing the proposing is more interested in marriage than he is in marrying you. Or he's more interested in the idea of you than he is in you. Either way, it doesn't bode well.

Chronically Unemployed Slow, Fast, or Medium Movers. Finally, beware men who can't seem to hold down a job or stick with an educational plan. Go ahead. Call me unromantic. But an inability to maintain steady employment or focus is often a sign that something else is wrong. The man may lack prudence. He may lack staying power. He may lack mental stability. It's not about the income or lack thereof. It's about what's causing the lack of income. And whatever it is, it generally won't confine its damage to a resume.

And if you can't? Then use the time he spends pursuing his passion to pursue one of your own. Knit while he watches the game. Read when he goes to train for his marathon. Master a new cake recipe while he's out hunting. There is a lot more to living than spending time with your guy. Live.

Don't Be Someone You're Not
This goes back to what we talked about earlier. Changing who you are is not the way to get a husband. That is, it's not the way to get the type of

husband you want. Anybody can pretend to love hiking for a few months. Anyone can keep their opinions to themselves one or two evenings a week. But eventually, the mask slips. The truth comes out. You're still the person you were, and the person for whom you've been playacting is sorely disappointed.

Dating isn't supposed to be an exercise in deception. It's not about convincing some unsuspecting soul that you're someone you're not. It's about slowly revealing yourself while receiving the slow revelation of another. Through prayerful discernment, time spent together, and living life in tandem for a little while, two people discern whether those tandem lives can become one life.

In order for that discernment process to work, however, both people have to be honest. They have to be themselves. You don't want to find yourself married to a different person than you dated anymore than the guy you're dating does. Besides neither of you will be happy in a marriage where you're expected to be anyone other than who you are.

Don't Do It

Don't. Don't half do it. Don't sorta do it. Don't start doing it. Don't even think about doing it. And you know what I mean by "it." If you don't or if you need some reasons why, just hold your horses and read on for a few paragraphs more. We'll get to "it" in the next chapter.

The Breakup: Because It Happens

Don't Try to "Just Be Friends"

That is, don't try right away. Friendship, or at least cordial relations, with exes is possible. But it takes time to heal, move on, and break old habits of relating.

Which means if you're the one doing the breaking up and he says he wants to still be friends, don't take him up on the offer. Do it for him. Out of love. He needs to understand that it's over, and agreeing to be friends won't help him with that. And if he breaks it off, don't you suggest being friends. That's not what you want. Don't pretend it is. Let go. Move on. If God brings him back at some later point, as a friend or something more, that's great. But in the meantime, God has something else for you. Go find out what it is.

For Your Post Break-Up Viewing Entertainment

Happy endings and chick flicks aren't always the best remedies for a broken heart. Try these movies and shows instead.

- "24" (Seasons 1-8): Terrorists, nuclear explosions, and nobody's relationship ever works out. Who could ask for more?
- "Miss Marple" (The BBC series): The sleuthing old maid who outfoxes criminal masterminds while she knits somehow manages to make spinsterhood seem like a cheery proposition. No small feat, that one.
- *Pride and Prejudice* (1996 BBC version): Yes, technically it's a chick flick and everything ends happily, but only after the heroine foolishly falls for the charms of the wrong guy and rebuffs the clumsy advances of the right guy. This breeds hope . . . and often reflects reality.
- *War of the Roses*: As a reminder that no matter how bad your breakup was, it could always be worse.
- "The Office": Because it's funny. And you need funny.

Don't Be That Girl

You know the one I mean. The girl who just can't believe it's over. Who still reads her ex-boyfriend's Facebook page every day, drives by his favorite haunts looking for his car, or checks Catholic Match frenetically to see if he's online searching for another woman. That's called stalking, and it's what crazy people do. But you're not crazy. You're a beautiful, precious, daughter of God. You're a catch. You deserve to be caught by someone who knows that. And that someone is not a guy you have to hound.

Don't Idealize or Demonize Him

No matter how it may seem in those first weeks and months after a relationship ends, the ex was neither Jesus Christ Superstar nor his arch-nemesis Lucifer. He was a man, with about equal amounts virtue and vice. He just wasn't the man for you. That's generally all there is to it. Which is why you need to let him go. Let it all go—the dreams, the anger, the desire. Start afresh and when someone new comes into your life, receive him as he is, without doing the old compare and contrast dance. Anything more or anything less, and you run the risk of missing out on something really good.

* *

Never Give up Hope

There comes a time in almost every single girl's life where she's had enough—enough dating, enough disappointment, enough bad endings. No matter how good she's been, no matter how well she's obeyed all the rules, it just never seems to work out. So she decides to give up. She stops looking, cancels her Ave Maria Singles account, and starts planning the shape of her spinsterhood.

But that's a mistake.

If you truly believe you're called to marriage, you can't throw in the towel. I know the dating scene is rough. I also know that the older you get, the slimmer the pickings are. Believe me, I know that. But there are still good guys out there—healthy, normal, working Catholic men who don't want to use you or control you. If and when the time is right, God will send one your way. You have to be open to that though. You have to leave yourself open—to getting hurt, yes, but also to being surprised by some totally unexpected, totally perfect gift from God.

Those are the basic rules. Naturally, there are more—don't let your jealousy show, designate your crazier insecurities as "inside thoughts," beware of intimate "prayer times" together, etc.—but my editors only allowed me so many pages per chapter, and we have hit the limit. Sorry. You get the general idea though. Keep it sane, keep it clean, keep it friendly, and you'll do just fine.

Even with the most comprehensive list of dos and don'ts, however, dating is still going to feel a bit like Charles Dickens' idea of the French Revolution: the best of times and the worst of times. No matter how old you are—twenty-two, forty-two, or sixty-two—there's no other single activity that can raise your hopes so high and dash them so low, both with such crushing regularity.

There's also perhaps no other activity for which we're so problematically programmed by the culture. TV, the movies, our former classmates' Facebook pages—all those can lead us to think that relationships and dating are supposed to unfold one way, and that if they're not unfolding that one way, we've done something wrong.

But again, it's the culture that has it wrong. Dead wrong. As Catholics, wanting good holy marriages that last (and wanting to make our way to a heavenly marriage that will last eternally), we can't buy into the culture's preferred mode of finding a mate. We need to do things differently, sometimes radically differently. There is a cost to that. Fewer options, fewer dates, fewer romantic thrills. That cost is nothing, however, compared to the cost of doing things the culture's way. And our payoff, when it comes, is exponentially higher than any payoff post-modern dating rituals can deliver.

In order to collect our full payoff for doing the dating thing right, however, there's one giant hurdle we still need to know how to clear: the Chastity Hurdle.

Ask the Single Girl

Dear Single Girl,

It's been ages since I've met an eligible Catholic guy, and I'm starting to despair. My friends keep telling me to sign up for one of the Catholic online dating services, but I'm not sure I'm comfortable with that. What should I do?

—Dateless in Seattle

Dear Dateless,

Trust me, I understand your hesitation. There can be something terribly awkward and odd about going online to look for a husband. It also feels decidedly unladylike to advertise your best qualities on a virtual billboard for marriage. Nevertheless, judging by the number of marriages that are made through them, sites like Catholic Match and Ave Maria Singles seem to be tools that God finds mighty handy. Let him use them in your life too. At least for a little while. Sign up and see what happens. Think of it as leaving a door open.

Do remember, however, that Catholic Match or Ave Maria Singles are tools for meeting someone, not tools for dating or having a relationship with someone. Which is to say, if you do meet someone, don't linger too long in the virtual world. Letters are better than on-line chats. Phone calls are better than letters. And dates over coffee are better than phone calls. The best and the worst bits of both of you can't be digitalized, which means online relationships (as opposed to simply meeting someone online) are fraught with peril. The longer your relationship stays confined to the online realm, the less honest it is. You're not getting to know the real person, just one side of him, the side he chooses to present. And that's a sure recipe for disappointment and heartache.

Likewise, keep your wits about you. An emoticon is not a proposal of marriage. It's a smile across a crowded room. Period. What you need to do is think of the first few emails, and even the first few phone calls like you would think about a random conversation with a stranger at a coffee shop or a party. In other words, keep it casual, chatty, and fun. Don't read too much into any one exchange and above all, do not start planning the wedding if a few phone calls go well. Remember, you have to wait for an actual ring to do that.

In sum, if you want to meet the man God has for you, you can't dictate the terms of how you'll meet. Leave all doors open, be careful, be incarnational, and let God do the rest.

Everything the Catholic Single Girl
Needs to Know About . . .

Sex, Chastity, and the Biological Clock

*Y*ou've got to love St. Augustine, for his honesty if nothing else.

When penning his spiritual autobiography, *Confessions*, the great Doctor of the Church recounted his decades-long struggle with chastity, a struggle that included his famous prayer, "Oh Lord, make me chaste, but not yet."

Augustine's prayer makes one thing clear: Chastity has never been easy. Not for the holiest among us and not for those of us considerably less sanctified.

But while chastity has never been easy, it's also never been quite so hard. Our sex-saturated culture has seen to that. We've got Hollywood, insistently and consistently, equating happiness and fulfillment with the quality and frequency of a person's sexual encounters. We've got the pornography industry peddling its wares on close to ten million different websites. And we've got a government happy to promote promiscuity through easy access to birth control and abortion.

Thanks to those folks (and many more), sex on the third date, if not before, has become the new norm in the secular dating scene. Which means that, nine times out of ten, agreeing to go out with anyone other than the nicest of nice Catholic boys is the same as agreeing to take part in a series of prolonged wrestling matches, both verbal and physical. And even some of those nice Catholic boys can surprise you.

Of course, there are only so many wrestling matches a girl and guy can endure before one of two things happens: the girl caves or the boy cuts. And that's that. In all but the smallest of Catholic and evangelical circles, an insistence upon chastity is the death knell of a relationship. Which is why a whole lot of nice girls have just stopped insisting.

It's not only external pressure, however, that makes chastity so hard. For us single women, chastity grows harder by the year. Exponentially harder. Not because of the culture. But rather, because of us. Because of what's happening inside us. Or, more specifically, because of what's not happening inside us.

That's right. I'm talking about the old biological clock, the physical imperative we women have to reproduce and reproduce often. It's real, it's powerful, and as a woman enters her thirties, it shifts her desire for physical intimacy into overdrive. What was always challenging starts to feel near impossible, and without quite knowing what hit you, you're suddenly entertaining thoughts you've never entertained before and confessing sins you've never confessed before. Not only do you have a harder time putting on the brakes when your date's engine gets going, but you find yourself struggling to not be the one starting the engine in the first place.

Back in the days when most women wed young and wed for life, this biological phenomenon didn't pose much of a problem. Now, however, with so many of us finding ourselves single well into our thirties and forties, it's become something of a game changer. Combined with all the pressure coming at us from the culture and the men we date or want to date, it's enough to make even the most chaste among us throw up our hands in despair.

But despair is always a bad idea. And despairing over chastity is a really bad idea. Chastity is not only possible, it's worth every struggle and sacrifice you have to make to attain it. Even the sacrifice of saying no to the beautiful, mysterious crinkly-eyed atheist from Starbucks who keeps asking you out.

Here's why.

Hip Spinster Sisters In History, Episode 2: Flannery O'Connor

She raised peacocks, wrote stories, and penned some of the wittiest letters ever written this side of the Atlantic. The stories are what the world remembers, but Flannery O'Connor's real greatness wasn't the ability to pen near perfect prose (an ability she had in spades), but her vision, her worldview. O'Connor saw the world through the eyes of a deeply faithful Catholic living in what she called the "Christ-haunted South." That vision fills her stories, infusing violence with grace, and sin with redemption. It also fills her extensive letters and essays, writings that reveal a woman who didn't just accept the trials and limitations God gave her—a fatal disease and quiet single life on her family farm—but found greatness through them.

Sex and the Catholic Church

When it comes to all things sexual, the Church has quite a bad rap in the culture. If you were just going by the opinions expressed on prime-time TV or the comment boxes at the *New York Times*' website, you would think the Church had something against sex, that she thought it a rather unsavory affair only to be indulged in by married couples and only when absolutely necessary.

Unfortunately, that reputation is not entirely undeserved. Not because of the Church's teachings per se, but because of how individual Catholics have understood (or misunderstood) the Church's teachings through the years.

For centuries, a good number of the Church's sons and daughters struggled to grasp and articulate the nature and purpose of human sexuality. On one hand, they knew it was ordained by God—there was after all that command to "be fruitful and multiply" (Gen. 1:28). But they also knew that sexual desire could be a mood-altering, mind-blowing, soul-destroying force. They knew its power, and they knew they needed to be on their guard against its misuse.

What they didn't always know was how to find the balance between the two, how to embrace the goodness of sexual desire while rejecting its darker temptations. They also didn't know how to express the need for that balance, in both thought and deed.

Some Catholics did know how, of course. But plenty of others did not. And their confusion or their inability to accurately articulate the Church's true teachings worked its ways into people's hearts and minds via pulpits, confessionals, and Catholic classrooms. That's the confusion that still lingers in the minds of Hollywood scriptwriters and on the pages of *The New York Times*.

In the twentieth century, however, at least in theological circles, the confusion started clearing up. The Church's understanding of sexuality didn't change: It deepened. Old teachings were remembered and new insights gained. The nature of the marital act as an expression of spousal love and an image of divine love, not just as a tool for procreation, was increasingly stressed. So too was the inherent goodness of a husband and wife's desire for one another.

Later in the twentieth century—between 1979 and 1984 to be exact—the Church figured out how to better articulate some of those insights and help Catholics understand more fully both the promise and danger of human sexuality. In essence, what she discovered was a new language, a new way of speaking about the Church's ancient teachings on sexuality and the incarnation that made sense to post-modern man.

That language is called the Theology of the Body. For it, credit goes mostly to one man: Pope John Paul II.

The Theology of the Body
Just in case you're not up to speed on what papal biographer George Weigel famously called a "theological time bomb," here, in brief, is what the theology of the body is all about.

It starts with the idea I mentioned in Chapter 2: The body expresses the person. Or, to put it differently, our physical bodies reveal invisible truths about our souls. They say something about who we are and what we're made for. They say lots of somethings actually, things about masculinity and femininity, motherhood and fatherhood, love and service, and much, much more.

Perhaps most fundamentally, they say we're made for union with another person. Like the *Iron and Wine* song tells us, male and female bodies fit together like "corresponding puzzle pieces." The one is made for the other, and when they come together in the right ways at the right time, their union is creative. It's life giving. It is, in a way, god-like, divine.

Along with that, the theology of the body makes it clear that we don't just have bodies. We are bodies. Our bodies aren't shells or husks that house the real person. Bodies are part and parcel of the real person. They are us, and as such what we do to and with our bodies has profound and lasting effects on our souls. Momentary actions can have eternal consequences.

From that, it follows that what we do with our bodies had better be good. That applies to all that we do in the body—how we eat, dress, work, exercise, dance, everything. It especially applies, however, to whom we give our bodies. If one of the most fundamental things our bodies reveal is that we're made for union, for communion, than the unions into which we enter will have more profound effects on our souls than just about anything else we do. They will either bring life, love, and joy to our souls. Or they will rip them apart.

Theology of the Body Basics

John Paul II's Theology of the Body

- ◆ was first given during the course of 133 Wednesday audiences delivered from 1979 to 1984;
- ◆ is an anthropology of what it means to be a human person, a union of body and spirit;
- ◆ teaches that the body expresses the person and reveals how men and women are made in the image and likeness of God;
- ◆ reveals that the one flesh union of husband and wife points to the life-giving communion within the Trinity;
- ◆ shows how using another person for our own pleasure violates the dignity of the human person;
- ◆ illustrates how the celibate life is a sign of the total self-gift we are all called to make of ourselves to God;
- ◆ calls all human beings to make a gift of themselves to one another in love.

That's not all the theology of the body has to say though. It also helps us understand how the marital act is an image of divine love and our eternal destiny.

God, remember, isn't *a* person. He's *three* Persons. "A family" is how John Paul II described him.[1] That's another way of saying that as Father, Son, and Holy Spirit, God is a communion of love. The Father's love is poured out totally and completely to the Son. The Son receives that love and pours it right back, eternally and completely to the Father. And that love is so real, containing everything both Father and Son have and are, that it too is a person, the Holy Spirit.

That eternal communion of love is, in a sense, what the marital embrace is ultimately about. When a man and a woman give themselves to each other, body and soul, completely and totally, permanently and irrevocably, they image, in a way, the communion of love in the Trinity. Their love echoes the life-giving love within the Godhead.

It also reveals an even deeper truth about man. We're not just called to union with another person: We're called to eternal union with God. We're called to spend eternity locked in a loving, life-giving, transcendentally joyful embrace with him. That's the beatific vision—pure ecstasy. And the act that our bodies most desire on earth is a hint, a sign, a foretaste of that for which we were eternally designed and destined.

Put all that together and what you have is the classic Catholic sacramental worldview, restructured and rearticulated for a culture plagued by a diseased understanding of the cosmos. It's a worldview that tells us that matter matters, that the physical not only reveals the spiritual, but is actually the means by which grace touches and transforms the spiritual. Fire and water, mud and spittle, bread and wine, they're all doorways for grace, entry points for the divine into our world and into our souls. So too are the bodies of husband and wife. That's one of the reasons why marriage is a sacrament. It's why sexual intimacy between husband and wife is such a holy thing. It's an act that shapes the nature of the relationship and can direct the souls of the lovers towards God.

---

1 "God in his deepest mystery is not a solitude, but a family, since he has within himself fatherhood, sonship, and the essence of the family, which is love." *Puebla: A Pilgrimage of Faith* (Boston: Daughters of St. Paul, 1979), 86.

Theology of the Body in Everyday Life, Part I: Live in the Real World.

The theology of the body teaches that men and women are called to live in communion with one another. That communion is a bodily thing, and our presence to one another should be bodily as well. It should be real, not virtual. So, limit time online—commenting on blogs, chatting on Facebook, or visiting virtual worlds. Also limit time in front of the television and time playing computerized games. Instead, spend real time with real friends doing real things. Throw a dinner party. Have a picnic. Pass a day together at the beach. Maybe go hiking. Play baseball. Or simply work with a friend painting a room, fixing a sink, or planting flowers. Just prioritize the real over the virtual, and discover grace in the most ordinary moments of life.

Sex and the Single Girl

The Good, the True, and the Beautiful

So what does all this have to do with you and that beautiful man from Starbucks?

Everything.

When you understand the Church's teachings on the human person and human sexuality, when you understand the theology of the body, the whole equation changes. Acts and feelings that you thought were negatives become positives.

To start with, you understand your own desires for intimacy are positive things. They're gifts from God that help you understand who you are—a woman made for union, for motherhood, and ultimately to be a partaker in the beatific vision. That doesn't mean those desires can be entertained, in mind or body, outside of marriage. As long as you're single they have to be checked, tempered, and re-directed. But the desires themselves aren't bad. They're a sign that you're a normal, healthy woman longing for the end for which God made you.

The theology of the body also changes chastity from a negative prohibition into a positive endorsement. You're not avoiding sex because it's so bad; you're avoiding it in the wrong ways and times because it's so good. By remaining chaste, you're witnessing to the beauty, the power, and the goodness of human sexuality. You're also recognizing that the marital act, in its power to unite two bodies, to bind two people together, and to be the channel through which a new life enters the world, is imbued with the sacred.

Think of it this way: You would never walk around town chomping on the Eucharist like you would a bag of chips. It's too holy and important of a thing to be received in any way, place, or time other than the way, place, and time the Church directs us to receive it. And while Christ's Body is on a whole different level of goodness than sexual intimacy, the same principle applies. To engage in it in any way other than the way the Church directs us to engage in it—in marriage, selflessly, charitably, reverently, with no barriers against the potential creation of life—is to commit a kind of sacrilege. It's to diminish the holiness of the act.

Theology of the Body in Everyday Life, Part II: Perform Corporal Works of Mercy

Use your body to care for the bodies of others. Feed the hungry. Clothe the poor. Visit the sick. Hold the hands of the dying. Take a child to visit the elderly. Build a home with Habitat for Humanity. Walk five miles to raise money for cancer research. Bake some cookies for the widow next door. Babysit a young couple's children so they can have an evening alone. Do any one of the thousand acts of charity that asks you to put your body at the service of those in need, and you'll be making a gift of yourself.

That's also why the theology of the body helps us understand that chastity is never about lines. It's not about how far is too far or how much you can get away with without needing to go to Confession. When you understand the beauty and meaning of sexuality, when you understand what a glorious gift it is, the goal can't be to abuse the gift as much as you possibly can without getting into trouble. Rather, the goal becomes safeguarding the gift, treasuring it and protecting it, until you can use it rightly.

The False, the Bad, and the Ugly

The goal also becomes protecting yourself—your dignity, your beauty, your capacity to love as God calls you to love.

Remember, the theology of the body teaches us that we can't do something to or with our bodies without also doing something to or with our souls. And when you become intimate with a man, you're not just giving him your body. Whether you realize it or not, you're giving him your soul. It won't come back to you untouched. It will be changed. You will be changed. And the nature of that change will depend on the nature of the act. It will depend on whether it was done in accordance with God's plan for human sexuality or whether it was done in violation of that plan.

To sin against chastity is to take a knife to your soul. The more you violate God's plan, the more slash marks you leave. And those marks don't heal easily or quickly. Only a tremendous amount of grace can knit the wounds back together, and even then, scars linger.

I'll be honest with you, I don't have those types of scars. I've been blessed and protected from inflicting these wounds on myself. But many of the women I know and love do. I've seen how they've suffered, both before marriage and long after. The ways in which they wounded themselves were different—some violated chastity before marriage with the man who would become their husband, some violated it with men who would not, some violated it once or twice, some violated it many, many times. Regardless of how different the situations were though, the effects of the violation are all of a piece.

There is guilt and shame. There is a diminished sense of trust. There is a belief—sometimes latent, sometimes apparent—that they aren't loved but rather used, even by men they eventually married. There are memories and feelings that haunt them. Many struggle to give themselves even now, when the place and time are right. They can't see the beauty of what they have, because of the ugliness of what they had.

For many, thanks to God and his grace, there has been healing. Like I said, however, scars linger. And not one of them, if they had it to do over again, would do things the same. They know the price they paid, and they know it was too high. They were ripped off, and their regrets haunt them still.

That's what you're signing up for when you give in to pressure from without or within. And that's the best case scenario. That's the scenario with grace, healing, and the love of a good man. Not everybody gets that ending. In fact, these days, most people don't. They just keep slashing and slashing, shredding their hearts and souls to bits, making it all but impossible for them to let God knit back together that which they've ripped apart.

He still can, of course. Sometimes he does. But the risks are too high. The costs are too high. And any guy who pressures you to bear those risks and costs is not worth it. He's just not.

Living the Theology of the Body

So how do we do it? That's always the question, isn't it? How do we live what we believe in the messy reality of the world?

Theology of the Body in Everyday Life, Part III: Dress Well

If the body expresses the person, then the clothes our bodies wear should likewise express our worth and beauty. In part, that means dressing modestly: Immodest clothes reduce a person to an object, an object defined by its sexual desirability. But, more than just dressing modestly, it also means dressing with style, with an eye to fashions that are flattering and attractive. It means dressing the body in clothes that aren't tattered and torn or shabby and shapeless. It means dressing like a woman if you're a woman, and like a man if you're a man. And it means dressing with dignity, showing your respect for others as well as yourself by not showing up at Sunday Mass in jeans, at restaurants in sweats, or at the grocery store in your pajamas.

Bind Up Old Wounds

It starts with healing. If you've messed up in the past, if you've given what you shouldn't when you shouldn't, you need to deal with that head on. The best way to do that is through the sacraments. There's no healing quite like Confession and the frequent reception of the Eucharist. Regular trips to Adoration also help. There is healing power in Christ's presence, and the more time you spend sitting before him, offering up every painful memory and every pang of guilt, the more he can help you.

Along with that, seek out a trusted female friend whom you can go to when you need to hear another voice reminding you of God's forgiveness and his plan for you. Most of us women are not made to keep what troubles us inside. Verbalizing fears and insecurities prevents us from rehashing them to death in our heads. Verbal assurances of our own worth, dignity, and beauty do the same. And there is no one who will listen or reassure you so well as a girlfriend.

Sometimes, however, even a girlfriend isn't enough. Depending on the depth and extent of your wounds, you may need to talk to someone else, someone who specializes in psychological healing. Just be sure, if you do, that the person to whom you talk knows, understands, and respects the Church's teachings on sexuality and love. If not, your conversations with them are apt to do more harm than good.

All that being said, it's important that you don't define yourself by your mistakes or sins. They can't become the defining paradigm of your life. You can think about them too much, and you can talk about them too much. When you do that, you give the devil a foothold, a way to pervert your own understanding of who you are and how God sees you. Accordingly, be careful about whom you share your past with and how much you talk about it. Don't treat life like a never-ending Oprah show. Your sins and struggles are not for everyone to know. They are especially not for male friends and men you're dating to know. They're for the man you marry to know, your confessor and/or counselor to know, and select female friends to know. No one else. Save God, of course.

Read Better Books Than This One
Seriously.

In this chapter I explained the theology of the body in exactly 711 words. That's about 120,000 fewer than John Paul II used and about 6 billion fewer than all the words others have used explaining John Paul II's words. The teachings contained within the theology of the body, not to mention all the implications and ramifications of those teachings, are beyond vast. People have spent the past thirty-plus years trying to digest them, and we're just getting started.

So do take it upon yourself to learn more about the theology of the body than the paltry summary I laid out in this chapter. There are books to read, talks to listen to, seminars and conferences to attend. There is so much to take in on this, and the deeper you go into John Paul's thought, the more your understanding of yourself, sexuality, and the world itself will be conformed to God's.

That being said . . .

Don't Read and Think Too Much About God's Plan for Human Sexuality
Just like you can talk too much about your own mistakes, you can also read too much about the Church's teachings on sexuality. It's important to know and understand them. But these are some pretty beautiful teachings. The more you recognize that, the more frustrating it can be when you don't get to enjoy some of their more exciting aspects. Trust me, there's nothing like sitting through talk after talk at a theology of the body conference, listening to speaker after speaker wax poetic about the joys of marital intimacy, only, at the end of the day, to go back to your room by yourself and sleep alone.

Fortunately, there's a lot more to the theology of the body than just sex. Like I said earlier, the theology of the body helps us understand how everything we do in the body matters—eating, sleeping, dressing, dancing, exercising, hugging babies, all of it. Focus on living those aspects of the theology of the body. Give up preservatives and foods that are bad for your body. Find your favorite form of exercise and stick to it. Learn to swing dance or waltz. Work on dressing in such a way that your clothes proclaim to the world the truth about who you are. Practice smiling to everyone you meet, even strangers you pass on the street. Do any one of the million-plus things you can do in the body that express truth, love, and goodness. The more you do that, the easier the chastity thing will become.

Theology of the Body in Everyday Life, Part IV: Hug a Child

Or hug a friend. Hug anyone you love. Smile at them too. Love is an incarnational thing. It requires a body—a body to look, touch, and speak care and concern, joy and pride, love and longing. That's why the beauty of the body comes not just from its size or shape. Most fundamentally, it comes from its ability to make you and your love concretely present, as well as to make it possible for you to give yourself away in love. Every time you let your love take on a bodily expression—through the look on your face, the touch of your hands, and the tone of your voice, you're living the theology of the body.

Surround Yourself with Like-Minded Friends

Living the theology of the body (and living the Catholic faith itself) is always something of a challenging proposition. But living it all on your own, without the support and encouragement of a Catholic community, is actually a dangerous proposition: It's one most likely to fail. So don't try. Keep company with other Catholics who can help you navigate the perilous roads of our secular and sex-obsessed culture. If you already have such friends, that's great. Treasure them. If not, seek them out. Sign up for the Wednesday Bible study at your parish or go to the monthly Theology on Tap Happy Hour in your town. Volunteer to teach CCD or feed the homeless with your parish's young adult group. If there is no young adult group at your parish, call the diocese. Ask to speak to their coordinator of Youth and Young Adult Ministry. Once you've got him on the line, find out what's going on diocesan-wide for singles and inquire about what other parishes in your area do have ministries for young adults. Then pay that parish a visit.

Also, remember that your Catholic friends don't have to be single friends. Married couples, as we'll discuss in Chapter Six, can make splendid support systems. So can older friends. Sometimes, the wisdom of a Catholic widow whom you befriend or an elderly resident in a nursing home can benefit you as much or more as the wisdom of a woman your own age. Likewise, keep in mind that friends don't have to be in the same state or even the same country as you to give a good pep talk and strengthen your moral resolve. Thanks to email, Facebook, Skype, and unlimited mobile-to-mobile minutes, reconnecting with your Catholic college roommate or cousin can be a quick and cheap affair. Naturally, personal presence is always preferable, but in a pinch a friendly afternoon phone call will do just fine.

However you find Catholic community, the point is simply to not go it alone, to not let loneliness give temptations to unchastity a foothold, and to not let friends who subscribe to the prevailing cultural attitudes about sex be the only voices you hear. As attractive as those voices may be, chances are they will lead you astray. And astray is not a place you want to go.

Be Your Own Thought Police

The desert fathers and mothers of old had a theory: They believed that the root of all our actions were our thoughts. In other words, they taught that good thoughts lead to good actions, and bad thoughts lead to bad actions. But they also recognized that we're not necessarily responsible for all the thoughts in our head. Some pop up entirely unbidden. Accordingly, they taught, since we can't be responsible for every thought we think, we must become responsible for what we do with those thoughts, for how we respond to them.

This is particularly true when it comes to chastity. There is no way you can control every thought and desire that enters your head. The same crazy hormones that make you weep when you see a pregnant woman in the store or hear a toddler cry out "Mama" on the playground, also make you think way more frequently than you should about the roughness of a man's skin or the strength of his hands. That's just a biological reality.

When those thoughts do come, however, they don't have to stick around. You can dismiss them. Not by beating yourself up about having them. Bad thoughts usually take that as an invitation to stay. Rather by saying, "Yep, this is normal. Thank God I have healthy desires. Now, about that project for work . . ."

Distraction really is key. Don't fight the temptation. Acknowledge it, hand it over to Jesus, then turn your attention promptly to something else. If the thoughts come when you're lying in bed, get up. If they come when you're unoccupied, occupy yourself. Get back to work. Call someone. Go do laundry. It's not easy to entertain impure thoughts and sort your whites at the same time.

It also helps to avoid occasions for impure thoughts. Don't read books with steamy love scenes. Likewise, avoid soap operas, racy movies, and television shows with too much smooching in them. Even in the ones where the level of smooching is reasonable, avert your eyes when the smooching comes. You don't have to be a dork about it and let everyone else in the room know what you're doing, but you still need to erect some sort of filter that keeps impure-thought-inducing images out of your head. No, you're not a guy, and no, you're not *as* visually stimulated as men are. But you've still got eyes and what those eyes take in affects what your brain dwells upon. Don't let them take in images of other bodies doing that which your own body is not yet allowed to do.

* *

Flex Those Muscles of Self-Control

A priest once told my friend Christopher, "Cookie today. Woman tomorrow." I love that. Somehow in four little words it manages to sum up the core reason for fasting and self-discipline. Exercising a little discipline now in small matters is the surest way to prepare yourself for exercising great discipline later in big matters.

Accordingly, if you want to steel yourself for facing down both your hormones and your date, do what the ancients have always done: Fast. Deny yourself today so you can deny temptation tomorrow. You can, like that wily old priest, fast from cookies. But it doesn't have to be food from which you fast. You can also fast from hitting the snooze button on your alarm clock, from buying new turtleneck sweaters, from complaining, or from skipping your workouts at the gym. Basically you can fast from just about any little indulgence or indulgent habit you have. The results are the same: You become more the master of your own actions. It's that mastery which is a prerequisite for the cultivation of any virtue, chastity or otherwise.

⁕ ⁕ ⁕ ⁕ ⁕ ⁕ ⁕ ⁕ ⁕ ⁕ ⁕ ⁕ ⁕ ⁕ ⁕ ⁕ ⁕ ⁕ ⁕

Get Out Before You Get Going and Stop Before You Start

The world's greatest experts at avoiding temptation of any sort—the Church's saints, fathers, and doctors—are all of one mind when it comes to the best way to avoid succumbing to our darker desires: Avoidance.

Avoiding temptation, you see, is a lot easier than running from it. If you're running from it, you've already seen it, and its power to stop you dead in your tracks is immense. If you avoid it, however, there's no temptation dogging your steps. You're free, at least relatively speaking.

This applies to cookies. If you don't buy or bake any, you're not going to blow your diet. It also applies to boys. If you don't put yourself in situations that can easily lead to sins against chastity, you're going to have an awful hard time sinning against chastity.

What are these situations you need to avoid? You're not fifteen and you can probably answer that as well as I can, but for argument's sake: Drinking too much at parties, on dates, or during evenings out; talking too long and too late in the car; talking too long and too late anywhere; sleepovers; laying down together; kissing laying down; kissing sitting down; maybe even kissing standing up; not to mention kissing with any portion of your clothing removed. And backrubs. Definitely backrubs.

Call me an old fuddy duddy. That's fine. These days, I'll take that as a badge of honor. Nevertheless, if you're serious about embracing chastity, you have to become a bit of an old fuddy duddy too. It's about the only guaranteed method of not messing up. You never have to stop what never gets started. Plus, it's a more honest way of relating. It's more true.

Again, all those desires for affection and intimacy and all the pleasure attached to affection and intimacy are not just there for the sake of our amusement. They're there because they mean something. They're signs of the human union and divine communion for which we're made. So when you touch someone, when you kiss someone, that too should mean something. It should be a foretaste of what's to come. It should be the beginning of the gift of self.

To share even a kiss with a man is to share breath. It is, for a moment, to share life. In the past, that was understood to be serious business, entertaining business mind you, but not pure entertainment. There is a distinction, and in our culture, we've lost that distinction. Along with it, we've lost a whole lot more.

Just so we're clear, I'm not saying you must make a hard and fast rule to never stay up late talking with your honey or never kiss a guy until there's a ring on your finger. Maybe you should, maybe you shouldn't. That's your call. I'm just saying exercise great caution in when, where, and how often you linger. Likewise, think before you kiss. Think about what a kiss means or should mean. Ask yourself if what you're doing with your mouth, your hands, and your body is in conformity with that. Is it in conformity with what's happening in your soul, with God's design for you, and is it in conformity with the nature of the relationship itself?

If it's not, why would you want to do it? Why would you want to be part of a lie? There may be an awful lot of fun in some lies. But there is no life in them. Nor is there any joy in them. Not real joy anyhow.

Theology of the Body in Everyday Life, Part V: Pray Like a Catholic

When Catholics pray, it's not just with our minds or spirits; it's with our bodies. We kneel, we genuflect, and we trace the Sign of the Cross on our foreheads, lips, and hearts. Our bodies are also the very means through which we encounter grace. The graces of the seven sacraments—from Baptism and Eucharist to Holy Orders and the Anointing of the Sick—all touch our souls after first touching our flesh—our foreheads, tongues, hands. Be aware of how integral your body is to your relationship with God. Let its movements mirror the movements of your soul. And bring it again and again into physical, personal contact with Christ in the Eucharist.

One last question. Is any of what I've written realistic?

The short answer: Heck yes it is. I wouldn't have written this if I didn't know for a fact that it was.

The long answer: It is if you want it to be. Living the Church's teachings on chastity is never easy, and few among us do it perfectly in every way, shape, and form. Probably no one does. Living them *almost* but not quite mistake free, however, is possible if you want it badly enough.

You have to ask yourself: What do I want more: A man or God? If you want the man more than God, if you want the boyfriend or the husband more than you want heaven, holiness, and all the joy that comes from being the woman God made you to be, then no, chastity isn't possible. You'll give in to him and to your own desires because that, at least in your mind, is the way to get what you want.

That really is the choice before you. When you're saying yes or no to the different types of men who ask you out, when you're alone late at night with a man who says he desires you more than anything, and when you're under the influence of soaring levels of estrogen, the question always is, who and what comes first? What matters more? What is more important?

Only you can answer that. Only you can make it possible for yourself to live chastity. There's grace, of course. But God's grace is never going to violate your free will. You make the choice for him, and he'll give you all the grace you need. Chances are, sometime, if not this time, he'll give you the man too. Because believe it or not, men who want God more than they want a woman, they're out there. And they're worth waiting for.

Ask the Single Girl

Dear Single Girl,

My mom says that I shouldn't be friends with men—that men and women aren't meant to be friends in the first place. But two of my closest friends from my college days are guys. I hate the thought of cutting them off, but I also don't want to do anything wrong. What should I do?

—Sally in Schenechtedy

Dear Sally,

I hate to say your mom is wrong, but, well, your mom is wrong. Men and women can most definitely be friends, and the annals of Church history tell us as much. There's Jerome and Paula, Teresa of Avila and John of the Cross, plus Francis de Sales and Jane de Chantel. In all those relationships there was a holy complementarity that we're called to imitate by cultivating chaste, respectful, and Christ-centered friendships with members of the opposite sex.

In fact, we need to imitate those friendships. Having a cadre of male friends is essential to surviving the single years. Guy pals move heavy things for us. They fix our toilets when they break.

And when there's no boyfriend in the picture, they accompany us to office Christmas parties and family weddings. They also teach us a lot about guys and are the surest check against us ever becoming "that girl"—the crazy, aggressive, pursuing, stalker chick. Perhaps most important, they help meet the need women have for male companionship and masculine wisdom, challenging us and amusing us in ways our girlfriends don't. And because they meet that need of ours in a healthy, platonic way, we don't find ourselves dating just to date, stringing along men in whom we're not interested, or settling for something less than what we really want. In other words, they protect us from many of the worst ways we're inclined to wound ourselves.

In order for that protection to work, however, the friendships do have to stay healthy. Keeping them that way comes with its own list of dos and don'ts. Do be honest with them about the nature of the friendship. Don't spend undue amounts of time alone with them. Don't get physical. Do hang out with them primarily in groups. And don't go revealing every peak and valley of your inner-life to them. When you need a shoulder to cry on, hunt down that girlfriend.

And what if one or both of you eventually decides you want something more than friendship? That could be good. It could be really good. As long as you're willing to listen to your mother tell you she was right and I was wrong every day for the rest of your life.

Everything the Catholic Single Girl
Needs to Know About . . .
Being a Career Woman

"What do you want to do with your life?" "Where do you see your career heading?" "What's next after this job?"

Twelve years ago I loathed those questions. And I loathed them for the very reasons I envied my guy friends when those questions were put to them.

When people asked them what they wanted to do with their life, they could answer honestly and without pause. Whatever they wanted to do—medical school, make it big with a lobbying firm, teach national security studies—was to them a simple matter of "a" plus "b" equals "c." They knew what they wanted, they knew what it would take to get there, and they planned accordingly.

I couldn't do the same.

In my early twenties I was a legislative staffer on Capitol Hill. I had a great job working for a great congressman and more responsibility than any twenty-three-year-old should rightly have. So, when people asked me what I wanted, I knew what they expected to hear: Speaker's Office. Law School. Think Tank. Something like that.

But that's not what I wanted. I wanted a husband, and I wanted babies. Politics was all well and good for the time. It was fun, challenging, and came with great bragging rights for my parents. I had no desire, however, to spend the rest of my life on the Hill.

That, however, presented me with two problems.

First, I never felt free to say out loud what I truly wanted. Second, I barely felt free to say it to myself. After all, I couldn't plan for motherhood like my male colleagues could plan for a legal career. What I wanted hinged on God sending someone into my life whom I could marry, and as we all know, God doesn't do that on command. I saw no clear path laid out for me, a path that automatically led to babies and homeschool co-ops. I felt neither capable of nor free to plan for Plan A. I could only plan for Plan B, and that meant not doing anything to jeopardize the career I did have—something that I feared boldly announcing my long-term lack of interest in politics would do.

But (and this was a big "but") in planning for Plan B, I also didn't want to do anything that jeopardized Plan A. I didn't want to put myself on a path that would get in the way of those babies and the co-op. I felt paralyzed and resentful. Why couldn't it be simpler? Why couldn't God give me Plan A now so that I wouldn't even have to bother with Plan B? Why did I have to plan for two realities? And how was I supposed to do that anyhow?

I'm not the only woman to have asked those questions. In this day and age, lots of us ask them. Then again, lots of us don't. Some of us have so totally bought into what the culture says we should want—a high-powered career—that we never consider how that career will jive with marriage and motherhood. Which is a mistake. Others among us so long for the husband and family that we don't consider seriously enough what we should be doing in the meantime. Which is also a mistake.

Why?

Because the former way of thinking can get you into an awful lot of trouble when the spouse and family finally do arrive on the scene. You can find yourself trapped in a job that's not family friendly or saddled with debt that's even less family friendly. And that's if you're lucky enough to have the family arrive. Plenty of women have been known to wake up one day, suddenly longing for a husband and children more than anything, only to realize that the decisions they made over a decade or more have seriously hampered their ability to find a husband and children. They pursued their career at the expense of their life. And they don't figure that out until it's almost, if not already, too late.

On the opposite end of the spectrum are the women who always assume the husband is just around the corner and stay trapped in a dead-end job they don't enjoy, which doesn't develop or use their God-given talents, or which won't provide for them sufficiently over the long haul—something that any job will have to do if Mr. Right continues to remain "just around the corner."

In the end, we don't really have a choice. Like it or not, planning for two realities is what we have to do if we're serious both about our desire to become wives and mothers and about our desire to serve God and be responsible in the meantime. We can't make the mistakes that our secular sisters do when considering questions of school and work. We have to simultaneously recognize both our desire for a family and the fact that what we desire may be a long time in coming. Then we have to plan accordingly.

But again, what does that mean?

* * * * * * * * * * * * * * * * * * * *

The Church's Call and God's Plan

Basically, it means when making educational and career choices we need to keep in mind the primary vocation to which we believe God has called us. Regardless of whether or not a potential husband is currently in the picture, if we think (or at least strongly believe) that our vocation is marriage, then we need to give that vocation some weight as we plan our professional lives.

Now, there are some folks out there who say something along the lines of what I just said, but mean something entirely different. When they say, "Avoid pursuing a career path that might get in the way of a future marriage," they mean, "Don't pursue a career. Any career. Or, if you must work, try not to be too successful at it. Mustn't intimidate potential mates, you know."

Since I'm a woman with a career, and a reasonably successful one at that, I am rather obviously not in their camp.

Nor is the Church.

Again and again, the Church has called for women to bring the feminine genius into the public sphere—to, as John Paul II wrote, "manifest the contradictions present when society is organized solely according to the criteria of efficiency and productivity," and help "systems to be redesigned in a way which favors the processes of humanization which mark the 'civilization of love.'" [1]

More simply put, the Church wants women to bring their feminine genius for serving, nourishing, and nurturing life into the marketplace, so that we can help transform our deeply messed-up society and build a culture of life. She doesn't want or expect us to sit on the gifts God has given us. She wants us to develop those gifts and use them, always in the home, but also in the world. God, at least according to Matthew 25, seems to want the same.

Matthew 25 is where you'll find the parable of the talents. In that parable, the master entrusts his various servants with some coinage, goes away for a while, and upon his return checks in with those servants to see what they've done with his money. The ones who used the talents wisely— who invested them and earned a profit—get a big pat on the back plus more responsibility. The one who wasted his talent, who hid it and didn't use it? It was off to the dungeon with him.

All this is to say that God did not give you a mind and any number of skills so that you could sit at home playing pinochle while you wait for Mr. Right. Nor did he give you those skills so that you can make "a job that won't intimidate a man" your number one career priority. He gave you skills so that you can use them to love and serve and build up his kingdom. Perhaps someday you'll get to do that as a wife and mother. For now, however, he expects you to use those talents in the world. And he doesn't want you to avoid doing that because you're worried no man will ever love you if you're successful. Regardless of what you do for a living, if your desire is to serve God through your work, the right guy will love you for exactly that reason. As for those who don't? Well, they aren't the right guy.

---

1 John Paul II, *Letter to Women*, 4.

> ### Thank You Note
>
> "Thank you, women who work! You are present and active in every area of life—social, economic, cultural, artistic and political. In this way you make an indispensable contribution to the growth of a culture which unites reason and feeling, to a model of life ever open to the sense of 'mystery,' to the establishment of economic and political structures ever more worthy of humanity."
> —Blessed John Paul II, *Letter to Women*, 2

The Vocational Hierarchy

Okay, now that we're clear on what I don't mean, what do I mean?

I mean first, that in discerning the degrees we pursue and the jobs we accept, God's will for our lives—not our parents' wills, not our professors' wills, not our boss's will, and not our culture's will—should be paramount in our decision making. Second, whatever jobs and degrees we decide to pursue, as well as the attitudes about our work that we adopt, should all ideally be, if not compatible with, at least not a hindrance to our desire to be wives and mothers.

In many ways this applies to all Catholics, men and women. We already talked some in the first chapter about secondary vocations. The idea, you'll remember, is that our secondary vocation is what we do on the path to holiness. And our job is part of what we do. Whatever our work may be—doctor, ditch digger, or diaper changer—it doesn't matter. That work is part of our journey towards heaven. It's one of the things that help us get to God.

But our secondary vocation, at least to some extent, is always at the service of our primary vocation. For a father of five who works as a principle of a high school, his work may help him develop the skills he needs to be a good administrator and enable him to serve his community. More important, however, it helps him develop the virtues he needs to be a good husband and father. It also enables him to serve his family, giving him the means to provide for and protect them. If, in any way, his job gets in the way of his primary vocation, if it diminishes his ability to be a good husband and father, then all the good he's doing for himself professionally or for his community matters less. A whole lot less.

The same holds true for us. Even if we aren't yet kissing ouchies by day and rocking infants by night, we still need to think long and hard before making career decisions that might make it difficult for us to rock those infants and kiss those ouchies. We also need to cultivate the right attitudes about our work, both for the sake of our sanity and for the sake of our ability to attract, meet, and marry a good man. Basically we need to see our work rightly—why it matters and why we do it—then plan our days and our professional lives in accord with that.

Working Saints

Holiness and a career aren't mutually exclusive. Just ask these saintly working women.
- St. Benedicta of the Cross (Edith Stein) (1891-1942): Philosopher and martyr
- St. Gianna Beretta Molla (1922-1962): Doctor, wife, and mother
- St. Wiborada (d. 926): Librarian and martyr
- Blessed Victoria Diez (1903-1936): Teacher and martyr
- Blessed Marguerite Bays (1815-1879): Dressmaker
- Blessed Maria Corsini (1884-1965): Professor, writer, wife, and mother

The Catholic Single Girl's Professional Development Plan

Okay, now it's time to stop dealing in generalities and get specific. How do we plan for an uncertain future without jeopardizing our shot at the primary vocation we desire?

Know That It's Not What You Do, It's How You Do It

In the world today, it's all about the "what": what our job title is, what company we work for, what salary we earn. For those among us who didn't spend our undergraduate days at schools like Franciscan University, the "what" is that which our education and background has usually conditioned us to care about. That's what those questions, "Where do you see yourself in ten years?" and "What do you want to do?" are all about. They're about "what" we do and, implicit in them, is the idea that the more impressive "what" we do is, the better our life will be.

But that's not how God sees it.

God isn't impressed by fancy titles or Ivy League degrees. He's impressed by how faithfully we carry out the work he's entrusted to us. That work always has eternal significance, even if it seems to be of little temporal importance.

So don't make the "what" the focus of your career plan. Don't let what's impressive or prestigious in the world's eyes (or possibly your parents') determine the career goals you set for yourself, the degrees you pursue, or the jobs you take. Discern what God is calling you to do and what he's equipped you to do, then do it. Do it well. Do it faithfully. Bring your femininity, your feminine genius, to bear on every task, great or small, and on every interaction you have with co-workers, clients, customers, and the cleaning crew. Whatever your work is, work for God. Make him proud. It's his opinion, and his opinion alone, that ultimately counts.

* *

Remember, Work Is Just Work

In other words, you are not your work, and your work is not your life.

Unfortunately, both those mindsets are far more common among us nice Catholic girls than they ought to be. Lots of us—myself included—work long and work late. We often neglect family, friends, and the carpet of dust on our living room floor in our race to meet the next deadline and surpass the next goal. We also fret and fuss about office politics, rapid advancement, and unreasonable benchmarks that we've set for ourselves—all while losing sight of what really matters, of why we're doing what we're doing.

As for why we succumb to that way of thinking? Well, it varies. Some of us have bought into the culture's ideas about what matters most and confused our lives and their purpose with our careers. Others among us know that work isn't the most important thing in life, but with the lack of anything (or anyone) better presenting itself, we act like it is. Sometimes we do that as a way of compensating for all that we don't have. Sometimes we do it purely out of guilt or a confused sense of obligation. After all, we don't have kids waiting for us at home. Why shouldn't we be the ones to stay late so that our co-workers with families don't have to?

Well, sometimes we should. Sometimes we should do the extra bit of work to help another out. But that can't become any more a way of life than staying late every night so that we can avoid going home to an empty house.

No matter what the culture says, you are not what you do. Your job is not you. Likewise, your job is not your life. No matter how much spare time your lack of a husband and family may afford you, a job cannot and should not be used to fill that gap. It cannot and should not consume your thoughts or your every waking hour. The more it does, the more you cut yourself off from all that brings lasting fulfillment—prayer, relationships, and well spent leisure time. Even the best of jobs can only be the poorest of substitutes for those things. It doesn't matter if you're running a home for special needs orphans in China or administering an AIDS hospice in Mozambique, if you're made for marriage, your work will not and cannot fill the space in your life that a husband is meant to fill. And no matter what you're made for, it will not fill the space in your life meant for God. Don't fall into the trap of thinking or acting like it will. A secondary vocation is just that—secondary.

Hip Single Sisters in History, Episode 3: Florence Nightingale

In Victorian England, nice girls from nice families didn't pursue careers. And they most certainly didn't pursue careers in nursing. The work of tending the sick was often left to the dregs of society and considered far more menial than being a servant. But Florence Nightingale changed all that. The daughter of a wealthy British landowner, Nightingale defied the wishes of her family, turning down multiple marriage proposals, and instead pursued training as a nurse. During the Crimean War, she led a team of women across Europe to care for British soldiers, and then after the war spent the rest of her life transforming the way nurses were educated and the way the sick were cared for. Through her work, Nightingale believed she was answering God's call. Those whose lives were saved by her and her methods agreed.

Seize the Day

On the flipside, you also don't want to make the mistake of thinking of your work merely as a way of killing time before your wedding.

First, you can't think of work that way because unless your birthright is a large trust fund or parents happy to indefinitely foot your pumpkin spice latte habit, you've got bills to pay. Right now and for the foreseeable future, you are your own husband, and you've got to provide for yourself as best you can.

More important, you can't think of your work as just "killing time," because in God's plan for you, this time of waiting was not unaccounted for. Again, he has work for you to do. Right now, not just when babies come. This is your opportunity to do that work and do it in a way you wouldn't be able to if you had a house full of toddlers.

For all the limits planning for two realities places on us, it also brings tremendous freedom. With no family to support now and no pressure to pursue a career path that will enable us to be the sole breadwinner for a half dozen mouths, we're freer than most men are to pursue our passion, even if it's not the most practical option. Which means you can take the job teaching theology in the Catholic high school and not worry too much about the less than stellar salary. You can go write for that newspaper, open your restaurant, or start an online stationary business with your best friend. You can sell all your worldly possessions and embark on a two-year evangelization stint across Ireland, or head south to Haiti and spend six months helping out at an orphanage. The options are almost endless. And that's because of, not in spite of, your present singleness.

You also should feel free to pursue those options without fearing that the husband will never come along if you do.

The thing is, if God is calling you to a certain job or educational path, it will not get in the way of the husband. Following God's will in one area can't block God's will in another. The missionary trip to China, the MA in theology, the nursing job in Boston—none of those are deal killers to marriage and babies if they (along with marriage and babies) are God's will for you. In fact, they may be how you get to marriage and babies. You might meet your spouse in China or end up taking a job in a parish where your future husband works. Alternatively, those career moves or grad school classes might simply be part of God's plan to make you a better wife and mother. If they're what he's calling you to, they very likely are.

So be fearless. Follow God wherever he calls you. This time in life is an opportunity that may not last and will not come again. Don't waste it.

Think Strategically

When making decisions about what degrees to pursue, jobs to take, or companies to work for, keep those yet to be conceived babies in mind.

This is something the culture and most colleges never tell us to do. So we don't. When we're eighteen and picking a major or twenty-two and looking for that first job, we're just thinking about what work we want to do, what interests us, sounds fun, or is simply available. Generally, we're thinking that way for one of two reasons. We're either assuming we'll want to continue working even after we've had children, or we're assuming that once the husband and babies arrive, we'll be able to chuck the career and be a full-time mom. Whatever the reason, the result is the same. Most of us never think about or pursue careers compatible with marriage and motherhood.

That has the potential to become one of our greatest regrets.

You see, when you're thirty-five, with babies at home and bills to pay, the challenges of balancing work and family look a lot different than they did at eighteen or twenty-two. You suddenly discover that the law school degree for which you worked so hard now means squat to you. All you want to do is stay home with your baby who needs you. Or you discover that for as much as you want and need to be home, you and your husband can't afford it. The mortgage must be paid, and one income just won't cut it. Quite often, women discover both realities at about the same time. They realize they have to choose between putting the babies in daycare while working long hours outside the home or living in a perpetual and mounting state of financial stress. Either way it tears them apart.

But there is another way.

A little strategic thinking early on can enable you, if it ever becomes necessary, to either work outside the home at a job that's family friendly or work from home, balancing income-generating obligations against family obligations on your own schedule.

Degrees in teaching and nursing have always been popular with women for just those reasons. They lead to jobs that can be done during shifts when kids are at school or asleep. So do other jobs in the medical field. My cousin Becky, for example, opted to go through a clinical training program after college instead of medical school. Now as a Certified Clinical Perfusionist, she goes in for scheduled surgeries—maybe two or three a week—then stays at home with her three children the rest of the time.

Likewise, there are some jobs that by their very nature lend themselves to being done at home. Those with degrees or experience in writing, media arts, design, and photography, as well as accountants, insurance agents, and certain types of lawyers can follow in the footsteps of centuries of wives and mothers who operated small businesses out of their homes. Once, working moms made lace or helped run the family farm. Today, they file their neighbors' taxes and sell handmade baby clothes on Etsy.

Similarly, more and more companies are increasingly happy to let trusted employees keep flexible hours or even work from home once babies arrive. My friend Cora is an engineer who, since giving birth to her three children, only goes into the office one day a week. The rest of the time, she works out of an office in her home while her children nap or play. Likewise, my neighbor Bridgett is a chemist and mother of four, who works remotely from her attic in Steubenville for a pharmaceutical company in Chicago. During the summers, when her chemistry professor husband isn't teaching, they go back to Chicago where she puts in time at the lab.

Obviously, not everyone has a skill set that allows them to run a business out of their home. Nor should everyone necessarily pursue an education or career path that is 100 percent compatible with family life. God may have other plans for you. A lot of us, however, do have gifts that enable us to be our own boss, and with a little careful planning, we can direct our careers in such a way that, if the need is there, we can both contribute to our family income and be home with our children.

As for how we do that, in some cases that will require looking for family-friendly companies with flexible policies to work for. In other cases that will mean focusing your work or studies in such a way that you'll one day be able to run a business from home. It might involve going back to school full-time or taking a few night classes at a local college. It's really not all that difficult with a little forethought, planning, and time. And time is exactly what God is giving you right now. Take advantage of that.

From the "Edith Stein Says It Better Again" File

"The nation...doesn't simply need what we have. It needs what we are."
—St. Edith Stein "Woman's Value in National Life," *Woman*

Do What You Love

None of this, however, is to say that "family friendly" should be your sole guiding light when making career decisions. God's will matters most. Along with that, so do your own interests and desires. All the women I mentioned above aren't just working at family-friendly jobs. They're working at jobs they enjoy. When they were still single they pursued their interests and used their God-given abilities to find work they liked. Then, with his help, they found ways to keep doing what they liked once children came along.

The children, however, never were a given. They can't be. Unfortunately, it's always possible that the family won't come. If they don't, you won't want to find yourself in a career you never would have chosen otherwise. If they do, you'll be a much happier wife and mother if you enjoy the job that's taking you away from your family. Work shouldn't be the reason you get up in the morning, but getting up in the morning is a whole lot easier if you don't dread your work.

Accordingly, when making decisions about school and work, consider what you love and what God seems to want you to do—what skills he's given you and what doors he opens. Also remember, just as God won't drag you kicking and screaming into a primary vocation that you don't want, neither will he drag you kicking and screaming into a secondary vocation you don't want. If you work with him and what he's given you, you'll find the right job . . . even if it takes a while.

Don't Mortgage Your Future to the Student Loan Corporation

Let me be clear from the start. School is great. Higher education is great. Graduate degrees are great. Or at least, they can be great. A lot depends on the cost. Which is to say, if you're thinking about law school, medical school, or that graduate degree in philosophy, there needs to be more questions asked in the decision-making process than "What do I want?" and "Will I be accepted?"

You also need to ask, "Can I afford it?" Because unless you're accepted into a fully funded program—tuition, living expenses and all—your degree means more than just a better or different job. It means loans, loans, and more loans.

When you're single or in your early twenties, that might not seem all that important. After all, education is an investment, and you'll have years to pay those loans down. Odds are, however, you're going to feel very different about those loans at thirty-five than you did at twenty-five.

Those loans, which don't seem like such a big deal today, will feel like a big deal on the day you and your husband decide you need to put off having children until your loans are paid down. They'll feel like a really big deal when you watch hundreds or thousands of dollars from your husband's paycheck go directly to Great Lakes Student Financing every month, not to buying a house, saving for retirement, or putting your kids into a good Catholic school. And they will feel like an enormous deal on the day you leave your newborn baby to go back to work because you and your husband can't afford to pay down your student loans with only one income.

I can't count the number of women I know trapped in jobs they don't want to be in or whose families live in near-poverty because of the burden of student loans. These women are lawyers, professors, doctors, and artists. In their twenties they did what everyone around them told them to do—pursue the degree, pursue the career, and not worry about the cost. Now they regret it.

If you can't get into a school that offers full or almost full funding, stop, think, and pray before you borrow. Make sure this is really what God wants for you. If you think it is, then look for other ways to help foot the bill.

If you're smart and careful, you can get the education you need without mortgaging your future to the Student Loan Corporation. You still might need to borrow a little, and borrowing a little is okay. It's borrowing a lot, borrowing sums that run into tens of thousands or even hundreds of thousands of dollars, that will come back to bite you. The truth is, most people—men and women—who borrow heavily to complete their education end up lamenting just how much they borrowed. The costs of repayment—financially as well as personally—are almost always more than they bargained for.

Own Your Future

Don't sign up for a future of indentured servitude to the Student Loan Corporation. Keep higher education debts down by . . .

. . . delaying your entry into the program for a couple of years so you can save more money.

. . . applying for a job at the university of your choice. Typically, if you're a full time employee at a school, tuition is free.

. . . taking more time to complete the degree and working to pay your living expenses while you study.

. . . looking for less expensive programs elsewhere. Sometimes, there's no substitute for a certain school. But most of the time there is.

As I've worked my way through this chapter, I've done so knowing that two lines of protestors may well be lining up to throw rotten tomatoes at me.

On one side are those who think the advice dished out in these pages is an anti-feminist throwback to a time when women were expected to do nothing more than stay home barefoot and pregnant (something which, in truth, I aspire to with every fiber of my being).

On the other side are those who get their dander up at the very idea of a woman taking on any work besides changing dirty diapers and settling squabbles between warring siblings (something which, again, sounds like a fairy tale happy ending to me).

The problem with both sides is that neither is being realistic. The one ignores the witness of working women all around them, women who not only want to be home but who know they *need* to be home, who know that their presence and guidance, not the presence and guidance of teachers, day care providers, or coaches, is what their children need most.

The other ignores the very real struggles of good Catholic families striving to be faithful to the Church's teachings on life and still pay their bills. For lots of those families, it's not a matter of simply adopting a simpler lifestyle and cutting out extravagances. For many there are no extravagances. There are just the basics, basics that can't be met on only one salary.

That same side also ignores the reality of the world in which we live, a world where most women can't remain at home with their parents until an offer of marriage comes along, where many women who want marriage won't necessarily get what they want, and where bills need to be paid.

The Church, however, ignores none of those realities. She understands the burden women and families face. She also understands the manifold gifts women have to offer society as intellectuals and professionals. She knows just how desperately the feminine genius is needed in the world today. That's the genius she asks all women who are able and willing to bring to the marketplace. That's the genius she asks you to bring to the marketplace.

For as long as we remain single, and perhaps after, doing what she asks is our duty. It's also our privilege, a chance to serve the God we love and grow in holiness along the way. Doing that in the right ways with the right attitudes is undeniably something of a balancing act that demands discernment, discernment, and more discernment. What's right and wrong for each of us is something no person or book (not even this one) can tell us. And no matter how perfectly we discern, our work is still going to feel like work. There is no perfect job. But that's why it's such an effective part of God's plan to make us perfect, which, remember, is the goal, husband or no.

Work and school, however, aren't the only things that should occupy our time while we're waiting for our husband to show up. We also need to make time for one of the best perks of the single years: Other people's children.

Dear Single Girl,

I'm trying to sort out my finances and was wondering: What's the best piece of financial advice anyone has ever given you?

—Broke in Boston

Dear Broke,

Good question, but do I have to pick just one? How about three?

First, save. Save a lot. In my twenties I ignored my parents' advice to do just that and decided to invest more in Ann Taylor dresses than my IRA. The IRA, I figured, was my future husband's responsibility. Not until I turned thirty did it sink in that the husband might not show up. And even if he did, I realized there was no guarantee he'd bring a cushy retirement account with him. Don't make the same mistake. Start squirreling away as much as you can right now. Have a hefty emergency fund in the bank and annually max out (or come close to maxing out) your contributions to your retirement account (and Health Savings Account if you have one).

Second, pay off your credit card in full every month. This nugget of parental wisdom I have been pretty good about, and boy am I glad for that. It's kept my credit rating high and got me a terrific rate on my mortgage. I also enjoy knowing that if I ever do get married, I won't be burdening my husband with my debt. In the days of old, women entered marriage with a dowry—cash or cows or corn pastures—that helped her and her husband start their married life on sound financial footing. The idea was that the more financially secure the couple was, the fewer problems they would have. That still holds water. Money is at the root of many a marital spat and not being deeply in debt at the start of your wedded life helps guard against your wedded life being unnaturally short. Unfortunately, lots of women (and men) now enter marriage with a dowry of a different sort—loads of credit card debt from their single days. Don't be that woman. Charge only what you can pay off each month, don't juggle more cards than you need, and consolidate whatever debt you do have onto a credit card with a zero interest introductory rate. Then work your hardest to pay that off in total before the introductory rate expires.

Finally, get good insurance: health insurance, car insurance, home or renters insurance, life insurance—you name it. As my dad always made clear to me, if you can insure it, insure it. I don't care how young or healthy you are. Tumors, car accidents, and fires don't send calling cards six months in advance of their arrival. That's why we have insurance: to protect us against the unexpected. So go find yourself a good insurance agent and ask him to help you pick the coverage he would want for his own daughter. You don't have to buy the Cadillac coverage, but you do need the best possible package you can afford. Remember, all your savings and good credit habits will be for naught if some emergency arises and your insurance doesn't cover the costs.

Following this advice does require some sacrifices. You'll definitely have to forgo an Ann Taylor dress or two (or twenty). But long after the Ann Taylor dress goes out of style, all that money you squirreled away will still be there for you.

**Everything the Catholic Single Girl
Needs to Know About . . .**

Married People and Their Children

For everything there is a season, right? A time to be born, and a time to die; a time to plant, and a time to pluck what is planted; a time for happy hours and a time for changing diapers. Or something like that.

But what happens when there's not? Or, more specifically, what happens when one of those seasons goes on and on and on, lasting much longer than it rightfully should? What happens when you're indefinitely stuck in a season that you have long since tired of and which many or most of your friends have long since exited? What happens when you're the last (or one of the last) showing up for those happy hours? What are you supposed to do then?

That sage old king in Ecclesiastes didn't exactly account for that problem, did he?

Well, lucky for you, I have. That's the focus of this penultimate chapter—adjusting to life when we're seemingly stuck in one season and most of the people around us have moved on to another.

If you're a wee young thing in your early twenties, you may not have the foggiest idea what I'm talking about. Stay single a few more years, however, and you'll find out. All those girlfriends who gather in your living room for wine and chocolate? They won't gather anymore, not unless they're gathering between the hours of noon and two on Saturday when their husbands are home and the children are napping. As for happy hours, well, those will take place in your friend's kitchen, and the wine she'll be downing will be more about soothing her toddler-frayed nerves than convivial conversation over a fine Bordeaux.

There's no getting around it: The longer we remain single, the harder it gets. And what makes it so hard isn't just our lack of a spouse and babies. It's also the spouse and babies that all our formerly single friends no longer lack. Life changes as friends marry and we don't. They move on to the season of diaper changing and we're left in the season of happy hours . . . alone.

Well, not quite alone. We can do what some singles choose to do. We can ditch our old wedded friends, seek out new single pals, and try, at least for a while, to avoid married people and their children. We can essentially entrench ourselves in Happy Hour Season.

Alternatively, we can retreat from the world altogether. We can choose to not pass "Go," not collect our $200, and head straight to Lonely, Miserable Spinster Season. We can hide out in our basement watching "Murder She Wrote," start perusing the Meals on Wheels menu, and buy cats, lots and lots of cats.

Or, we can adjust. We can treasure whatever single friends we have left, befriend new singles as opportunity presents, and, in the meantime, lean into the life God is giving us now, at this moment, married people and all. Essentially, we can embrace a season that is neither Happy Hour Season nor Lonely, Miserable Spinster Season. I call it the "Hanging out with Married People and Their Kids" Season.

I know, the title isn't great. I'm working on a new one. In the meantime, however, this one will have to do. And titles aside, the season itself is actually a pretty darn good one. We get to keep our old friends, make some new ones, laugh a lot, learn a lot, and snuggle with babies galore. Yes, there is less gallivanting about town in this particular season, but the joy, the depth, and the wisdom to be found here beats the pants off Happy Hour Season.

Don't believe me? Read on.

Obstacles to Entry

Before we talk about all that single people and married people stand to gain from close friendships with one another, let's be clear about one thing: Forging or maintaining relationships with married people is difficult. Not impossible, but difficult.

In truth, there are all sorts of perfectly valid reasons why singles everywhere choose to hang out at bars after work rather than dine with toddlers. At the top of that list are some basic problems of scheduling.

You and I both know that the Catholic single life is not all nightclubs and weekends in Bali. *Sex in the City* it ain't. (Nor would we want it to be.) But the shape of our days and nights is still awfully different from those of our married friends. Unlike those in the Diaper Changing Season, we're not juggling work and toddlers (or warring teenagers and toddlers or homeschooling and toddlers). We have the laundry of one person, not five, to do. Plus we get to decide all by ourselves if we're going to spend one hundred dollars on U2 tickets or tuck the cash away for a rainy day. When it comes to how we spend our time and money, we're accountable to no one. They are.

Likewise, when friends get married, they're less available to us than when they were single. Then, when they have kids, they're a *lot* less available. They can't always be there for us when we need someone to talk us down from a fight with our boyfriend: Their two-year-old with the flu must come first. Similarly, naptime gets in the way of shopping trips, husbands get in the way of late nights spent watching BBC period dramas, and hospital bills from their last pregnancy get in the way of dinners out. Spending time with them is simply more difficult—and in some ways, less fun—than it used to be. So we don't. Or at least, we don't as much.

But it's not just scheduling problems that lead some single people to plant their feet firmly in Happy Hour Season. It's also what's said . . . and what's not said.

In general, neither single people nor married people are very good at speaking the other group's language. We singles often say stupid things about marriage and raising kids ("You're still breastfeeding at how old?") and they, God bless their well-intentioned hearts, say the stupidest things about dating and the single life. They corner us at parties and ask what's taking us so long to find a husband. They wax rhapsodic about how nice it would be to be single with so much time and so few problems. They go on and on about their children and their children's children, oblivious to the knives they're driving into our childless hearts with every word they speak and story they tell.

Sometimes, it's enough to make even the most married-people-lovin' among us run screaming straight into the arms of the first single person we meet.

Unfortunately, that's not even the worst of it. Maybe the number one reason so many of us single people are wary of the Hanging Out with Married People and Their Kids Season has nothing to do with married people and everything to do with us. Often, our avoidance is about our sorrows, our fears, and our insecurities. It's about how it can feel to spend time with couples living the life we so desperately want to lead. In short, it hurts.

For all those reasons and more, it's understandable why many single women (and men) start looking for a new single best friend when their old best friend gets married. It's also understandable why, when a new baby arrives at our former roommate's house, we call and visit less often. And it's totally understandable why we avoid gatherings where we'll be vastly outnumbered by married people and their children. We just don't seem to fit in.

But while avoidance may be understandable, over the long term, it's not really possible. The longer we're single, the more married people we know. By the time we're in our thirties, they're everywhere. Our cousins and siblings, college roommates and co-workers, neighbors and fellow parishioners—we simply can't avoid them like we could in college and just after, nor can we keep making new single best friends indefinitely. Married people must be dealt with and dealt with rightly lest we become the creepy old lady in her fifties hanging around new college grads at the local Applebee's.

Even if you're cool with being that creepy old lady, however, you shouldn't be. There's way too much fun to be had in the Hanging Out with Married People and their Kids Season, and there's way too much to learn that will help you successfully navigate your own Diaper Changing Season should that day come.

Think Before You Speak

It's inevitable. Your mom, your neighbor, the nice lady in the front pew at church—they're all destined to say the wrong thing at the wrong time about your single status. When they do, bursting into tears is not an option. So what do you do?

They say: "Better hurry up and find that husband, time's a-wasting."

You might think, "What am I supposed to do? Stand on a street corner and pop the question to every third man that walks by?" . . .

But you say (with a smile), "It sure is. Pray for me."

They say: "Single people have it so easy."

You might think, "Says the woman who's never worked to pay a mortgage, mowed a lawn, or fixed a clogged sink in her life." . . .

But you say (with a smile): "I'm very blessed. Pray for me."

They say, "Don't be too picky. There's nothing wrong with settling for someone less than Prince Charming."

You might think, "So, how's that working out for you?" . . .

But you say (with a smile), "Well, pray the good Lord sends someone."

They say, "God often waits to send us someone until we've worked on ourselves a little more."

You might think, "So why didn't he do that with you?" . . .

But you say (with a smile), "Thanks. Pray that I'm able to do that."

Marriage 101

Occasionally, the lessons we learn from our married friends are exactly the lessons they think they have to teach us—lessons about finding and snagging a mate. More often, however, the best lessons they have to teach us are the lessons they're not trying to teach us at all, lessons that come to us through the witness of their lives.

Perhaps the most fundamental of those lessons has to do with the truth about marriage.

Whether we realize it or not, that truth is one most of us need to learn. Not just because we're fed a steady diet of lies about marriage by the culture, but also because precious few of us grew up in homes where our parents' marriages modeled all the Church says marriage should be. Many of us have no first-hand experience of what healthy, holy Catholic marriages look like. Which is where our friends' marriages come in. When those marriages are Catholic marriages, where both parties are committed in principle, if not always action, to the Church's teachings, we get to see what many of us missed growing up. We get to see sacramental grace at work.

Over time, our friends' marriages can be the antidote to every wrong conception of marriage Hollywood or our parents have given us. We can see in their lives that marriage isn't a sitcom, where major life crises are resolved in thirty minutes or less, nor is it a tragedy, always fated to end badly. Rather, we can see that marriage is God's way of making two people holy. And there are no easy paths to holiness. This one, like all the others, is hard—painful even. It requires constant giving, constant self-denial, and constant forgiveness. It requires loving someone when you don't want to love them, when they've hurt you, neglected you, even cheated on you. It requires that you temper your tongue and your will, dying to yourself with every coupon you clip, dinner you cook, and Christmas you spend at your mother-in-law's.

As our friends do that, we're privileged to see holiness blossom in them. As we watch them forgo a night out with the girls so they can stay home with a depressed husband, abandon hopes of a family vacation so they can pay the latest round of doctor's bills, and skip "Dancing with the Stars" so they can do their family's laundry, we witness their rough edges soften, tempers mellow, and charity deepen. We behold transformation, and in that we learn that marriage does indeed do what it promises.

We also learn from our married friends what makes bad marriages bad and good marriages good. We see how an inability to offer criticism in love and accept criticism with humility leads to a breakdown in communication.

We see how a breakdown in communication leads to misunderstandings, how misunderstandings lead to confusion, and confusion leads to betrayal.

Conversely, we see the difference it makes when a couple prays together and goes to daily Mass as often as possible. We see the fruit that's borne when couples don't run from suffering—from enduring the pain of another miscarriage, a prolonged illness, the loss of a job—but instead place themselves and their sorrow completely in God's hands. We also see how a little humor helps when a husband crashes the car or when an entire family is up all night with the stomach bug.

Above all, from our married friends we discover that marriage, in and of itself, isn't going to make us happy. It can contribute to our overall happiness, but it's not the cure-all for insecurity, loneliness, isolation, guilt, or fears about the future. Every time a married friend frets to us about her weight, worries aloud about her children's safety, complains about having no one to talk to during the day, and confesses that she feels miles apart from her husband, we can't help but discover that truth and the reason behind it.

That reason, of course, is that no matter how great our friends' husbands might be, none of them are Jesus. There's only so much love a man can give. There's only so big a hole a man can fill. The real determining factor in a person's happiness isn't a ring on their finger. It's a relationship with Christ—Christ in prayer, Christ in Confession, Christ in the Eucharist. That relationship, and only that relationship, can truly heal insecurities, stave off loneliness, and end all worry and guilt. Learn that lesson now and not only will you be a lot happier all your single days, but you'll be a lot happier all your married days as well.

That's true of all the lessons about marriage our married friends have to teach us. The more we learn the truth about marriage now—about what it is, what makes it work, and what we should and should not expect from it—the better we'll be able to apply those lessons should a husband ever come our way. We will have a happier and holier marriage and a happier and holier life for the lessons we've been privileged to learn through them.

We'll also be a lot more knowledgeable about the nuts and bolts of raising a family.

On Married Men and Unmarried Women

So what do you do when one of your oldest guy friends gets married? Can you stay friends or do you have to hug him goodbye on his wedding day?

The answer depends on his wife. If she's comfortable with you, then chances are good the friendship can survive. If she's not, you need to exit stage left. Even if the friendship survives, however, it will need to survive differently.

Essentially, you need to become her friend more than his. She needs to be the one you primarily speak with at parties, invite to gatherings, and call up if you need something. The same goes for all the married people in your life (except for maybe your brother). The friendship with the woman, conversation with the woman, and time with the woman always has to come first.

You can and should, of course, work to get on well with the married men you know—your friends' husbands, co-workers, and longtime male friends. But there can be no exclusive, close friendships with married men. You can't hang out with them alone, call them up just to chat, or go to them with your personal troubles. Not only does doing so raise red flags in the wife's mind, but it also sows the seeds of infidelity. For one of you, if not for both of you, it can become, at the very least, a near occasion of sin.

Don't think just because you're both Catholic that you're immune to such sins. You're not. No one is. Do whatever it takes to avoid learning that lesson the hard way.

Babies 101

No matter how mysterious and beautiful family life seems from afar, up close and personal it's a whole different story. It's still beautiful, of course. But it's beautiful like the tree in your backyard—craggy, quirky, and real—not beautiful like a Monet painting in a museum—all gauzy pastels, sunlight, and blurry brushstrokes.

And mysterious? Well, only in the sense of "It's a mystery these people haven't killed each other."

As for the rest, there's little mystery about it. The more married couples you befriend, the more you're exposed to the nitty gritty of sex, pregnancy, and parenting.

Sometimes that means you hear details you really, really don't want to hear. (If the words K-Y jelly come up I recommend developing a sudden urge to visit the Ladies' Room.) Most of the time, however, it means you'll get valuable firsthand knowledge about parenting for which no book can adequately substitute—how to deal with temper tantrums, get babies to sleep at night, calm hormonal teenage crying jags, do battle with picky eaters, negotiate peace agreements between siblings, potty train toddlers, and effectively bribe children between the ages of two and twenty to do what they ought.

Spend enough time with married people and you'll also find yourself capable of speaking at length about the "womanly art" of breastfeeding and the upsides and downsides of attachment parenting. You'll be able to discuss the merits of homeschooling versus Catholic schooling with seasoned veterans of those debates, as well as know in great detail what's wrong and what's right with Dr. Dobson, what to expect when you're expecting, and how to tell, without even taking your temperature, when your body's ripe for conceiving a baby.

Along with that, you'll witness first-hand the myriad ways that families can incorporate the faith into their daily lives. You'll discover how celebrating feast days and name days, setting up a family altar, baking Resurrection Bread, and hosting "Jesse Teas" conveys the truth to little ones about God and the Catholic life in ways no textbook ever will. You'll be well versed in what programs such as the Catechesis of the Good Shepherd, Little Flowers, and "Faith and Life" have to offer. You'll know the lyrics to every VeggieTale song yet produced, and you'll find yourself the proud possessor of multiple tricks for managing restless toddlers during Mass.

Should you ever find some fellow whom you're inclined to marry, all this knowledge will make you a vastly better wife and mother. Should you remain single all your life, you'll be one of the best-trained babysitters on the market . . . not to mention a source of sound advice for other young women who happen to cross your path.

But no matter what the future holds, every hour spent in the company of couples with kids is worth it for one reason and one reason alone: the kids.

Conversational Dos and Don'ts

When striking up a conversation with a newly introduced Catholic mom . . .

- *Do* ask her the names, ages, and the first words of each of her children.
- *Don't* express shock or horror if (a) she's breastfeeding her four-year-old, or (b) mentions the words "family bed."
- *Do* tell her how beautiful, clever, and charming her children are.
- *Don't* ask her when she's due, no matter how pregnant she looks. (The line between "about to have a baby" and "recently had a baby" is a fine one.)
- *Do* offer to hold the crying baby so she can get some food or visit the ladies' room.
- *Don't* ask her why she is or isn't breastfeeding.
- *Do* respond to her every comment about parenting choices with, "I'm so glad you've found that works for you."
- *Don't* go on and on about your fabulous career/exciting travels/busy social life/size four figure . . .

A Child's-Eye View

More than any lesson about marriage or parenting that married people can teach us, the best and greatest gift we reap from our relationships with them is the gift of their children—their children's time, their children's love, their children's wisdom. That is the ultimate payoff for signing up for the Hanging Out with Married People and Their Kids Season.

Spending time with families—especially good Catholic families who tend to produce babies in spades—provides us single women with the only known (albeit temporary) antidote for our increasingly frustrated, wanna-be-mommy hormones: a ready supply of babies to kiss and snuggle. Holding a sleeping baby is like eating chocolate . . . only better. And a five-year-old who throws herself into your arms with cries of delight when you walk in a room generally does more for your self-esteem than any number of come-ons in a crowded bar.

Those same little ones are often as adept at amusing as they are at loving. Kids do indeed say the darndest things, and as the single friends of married people, we get to share in the fun. Case in point: My five-year-old niece Emma, who when asked by her exasperated mother, "Where did we get you?" solemnly responded, "I'm not sure, but I'm guessing Target."

More than kisses and laughter, however, there's great wisdom to be gained from friends' little ones. They see the world with an unvarnished eye, and in that, they teach adults willing to learn from them how to do the same. They teach us that the only proper response to a snowstorm is snowball fights and hot chocolate. They teach us that skirts are meant to twirl out in wide arcs when we spin in circles. They teach us to run, not walk, on the first sunny day of spring, that worms are miraculous wonders straight from the hands of God, and that flowers should be given liberally to everyone we love. Basically, they teach us the art of joyful living.

To children, joy comes far more naturally than it does to us sober grown-up types. Like with most things, it's a question of vision. When rain falls, adults see slippery roads and disruption to travel plans. Kids see frogs and giant puddles to jump in. When ballet tickets are in hand, we see the hassle of fighting traffic. Kids see bodies that fly. We see the practical. They see the beautiful. We grown-ups need to see what we see. But we also need to see what children see. And if we're open to it, time spent in their presence enables us to do just that.

Somehow, mysteriously, when children feel wonder, the adults around them can feel wonder too. When they see beauty, we can see beauty too. When they take delight in a ball of yarn, a red-gold leaf, or freshly baked batches of cookies, we can take delight in those things too. Their joy is contagious. It's almost as if they're little conduits of grace, miniature channels through which God reorders souls, giving back just a bit of the joy that years of sin and sorrow have taken from us.

To give that up because it sometimes hurts, because their parents (and us) are occasionally prone to saying stupid things, or because scheduling time together is just plain hard, is a mistake, a tragic mistake, and those who make it might spend a lifetime regretting it. Remember, someday God may give you children of your own. But he might not. Your friends' or siblings' children might be the only children you're given to love. Don't pass this opportunity by.

Borrowing Other People's Children

Most of the fun. Only a little of the work. Do it and do it often. It's one of the single life's best perks.

- Invite your friends' children (and their parents) to your house in December to help you decorate your tree.
- Treat your nieces or goddaughters to an annual trip to the Nutcracker.
- Host an Easter Egg hunt in your neighborhood.
- Take your friends' five- and seven-year-old on a nature walk in the fall.
- Host a tea party: dress up clothes optional.
- Invite friends' pre-teens or teenagers to help you get ready for a dinner party, paint your garage, or plant a garden. (With Mom it's work. With you, it's being treated like an adult.)
- Volunteer to take a friend's kids sledding or to the park.
- Give your godchildren gift cards to Barnes & Noble for their birthday, then go with them to use the card (and drink hot chocolate).

The Single Friend's Gift

This is all sounding pretty mercenary, isn't it? Lessons in marriage, tips on childrearing, babies to kiss and snuggle. Are we the only ones to get something out of the Hanging Out with Married People and Their Kids Season?

Hardly.

Married people come out of this pretty well too. They need our friendship as much as we need theirs.

I know it doesn't always seem like that. After all, they have the spouse, the kids, the home of their own—what can we possibly have to give them? Don't they already have it all?

The answer is, "No they don't." There are many gifts you can give them. Starting with your help. They definitely need that.

As single women we might not have loads of free time, but the free time we do have is often of the more flexible variety. Rearranging our schedules to accommodate a married girlfriend in need is typically easier for us than it is for a woman with six kids. We can serve in ways she can't.

As such, we come in mighty handy when a new baby is born and meals need cooking or errands need running. We come in equally handy when bedrooms need decorating, kids need watching, and gardens need planting. And there's no better friend to take along on an outing to the park than a single friend. We bring with us two hands and no children of our own to occupy them.

In addition to our help, married women need our ears.

At 5:00 in the afternoon, when all hell is breaking loose and her husband isn't home yet, the married woman needs someone to talk to who is not enduring her own 5:00 toddler hell.

That would be us.

When she is sick to death of her children, other people's children, and the mere discussion of children, the married woman likewise needs someone to talk to who is guaranteed not to broach the subject of potty training or co-sleeping.

Again, that would be us.

Most importantly, when she's struggling in her marriage or feeling guilty about certain parenting decisions, the married woman needs someone to talk to who is not in competition with her for the "Wife and Mother of the Year" award. In other words, she needs someone who can hear her confession but who is not doing marriage and motherhood better than she is.

That is very much us.

Single women, whether we realize it or not, have a great deal to offer married women—our help, our time, and yes, even our wisdom about men and babies. Despite our single status, many of us can honestly lay claim to both.

We also have one more gift to offer, the most important gift of all, the gift of ourselves. All the reasons our friends have always needed us—our company, conversation, sympathy, humor, interior design know-how, and killer fashion sense—are reasons our married friends need us too. Their love for us doesn't change when they marry. Likewise, the married women we meet are just as capable as single women are of appreciating the unique unrepeatable wonders of God that we are. Sometimes, marriage even makes them appreciate us more. From what I'm told, there's nothing like living with a man to make a woman long for female companionship and conversation. As we've said before, men are great, but even the best of husbands is no substitute for a girlfriend.

Rules of Engagement

If and when the occasion arises, how exactly does a nice, single girl like you go about embarking on this new season in life?

As always, I have some tips.

Be flexible and available.
This is where it starts. We can't expect to enjoy the same leisurely nights out on the town that we enjoyed with our friends in their pre-kid days. So, if spending time with them means doing yard work on a Saturday at their place, then grab a rake and go. And if plans for Friday night fall through because little Lucy has a fever, patiently wait for the next available night. See it as a matter of priorities, as a question of what's more important: spending time with friends or trying out that fabulous new Thai restaurant?

Look for opportunities for service.
Our singleness is a chance to serve those we love, and it's not hard to find ways to do just that. Moms need help all the time. Let me repeat that. All. The. Time. They will rarely turn us down when we offer to cook a meal, babysit, or run some errands. And even if they do, the offer will still be deeply appreciated and perhaps taken up at some other time. What it comes down to is this: If we single women can't find ways to care for our married friends and their families, we're not trying hard enough.

Pursue.
Singles need to assume a good part of the burden of nurturing friendships with families. It's not always easy for a nursing mother with three toddlers running around the house to call up her friends for long chats or even keep track of how long it's been since you last talked. So don't let your feelings get hurt if your old roommate doesn't ring you up as often as she used to. Just remind yourself that she's adjusting to life as a new mother and ring

her instead, offering to play with the little one while she gets some laundry done. You could offer to do the laundry . . . but I'm not going to tell you to do what I wouldn't do myself.

❖ ❖ ❖ ❖ ❖ ❖ ❖ ❖ ❖ ❖ ❖ ❖ ❖ ❖ ❖ ❖ ❖ ❖

Do a Little Shopping and Redecorating.

I'm not talking purchasing new couches and Pottery Barn kids' kitchens, but your friends will feel considerably more comfortable bringing their brood over to your place if they're not worried about little Benjamin shattering your china or sticking his finger in a socket. Pick up a few toys at a yard sale, toss your old bridesmaid dresses into a box for playing dress up, and move anything breakable or valuable out of a toddler's reach. Also, when you're alone, practice saying the words, "That's okay. Everything breaks sometime." That, more than anything else, is what your friend needs to hear when her rambunctious two-year-old uses your grandmother's china plate as a Frisbee. At least, that's what she needs to hear if you want her ever to come back.

Shopping List

Don't rush out and buy these items all at once, but over time, the more of them you acquire, the easier hosting little visitors will become. And yes, I do have them all by now. My friends have lots of kids. LOTS of kids.

☐ At least one booster chair (I have three);
☐ A pack n'play;
☐ Sippy Cups (you can never have enough);
☐ Child-friendly utensils, plates, and bowls;
☐ Bibs;
☐ Netflix (instant streaming of thousands of kids' shows straight to your TV);
☐ A dress up box (compiled on the cheap with gauzy fabric remnants, ribbons, old hats, discarded suit jackets, and old bridesmaid's dresses . . . that you never have worn again);
☐ A toy box (compiled on the cheap with donations from friends . . . there's always toys they want to get rid of);
☐ Fancy Nancy Books . . . for you, as much as the little girls;
☐ Old blankets (for impromptu fort building);
☐ A child gate . . . so you don't spend the rest of your life feeling guilty about the concussion little Charley got on your stairs.

Keep Healthy Boundaries.

It's okay to say no when friends ask you to babysit, and it's more than okay to set rules that other people's children need to abide by when they're in your house. In fact, it's necessary. Just because you're single doesn't mean you're not overwhelmed, busy, and stressed too. You can't always be available to serve, and your friends need to know that. Also, your acts of service should be given willingly, not resentfully, and the time your friends and their children spend at your house should be a joy, not a burden. If you never say no, however, or let the babes run roughshod over your bedroom, neither will be very possible.

Don't Criticize Their Spouse.

It's not your job to point out all the things that are wrong with their husband. Nor is it your job to take sides in disputes. Your job is to be on the side of the marriage—supporting it, defending it, praying for it. Obviously, if there's real abuse or endangerment, you need to speak up, firmly and with love. But save for those occasions, keep your opinions to yourself. Offer your friend sympathy when it's called for and agree with her (gently) if her spouse's behavior truly is problematic. But then direct her back to her husband. Tell her to talk to him about the problem. Even defend him if necessary. This may feel counterintuitive, but no matter how just your criticisms of him might be, in the long run your friend is likely to resent you for it and he's likely to hear about it. Neither of which bode well for future friendly relations.

Give Lots of Reassurance.

Like I said, being a wife and mom doesn't automatically make you less insecure. Often, it just gives you more to be insecure about. That's why the best gift you can usually give a married friend is reassurance. Don't critique her children or her parenting decisions. Just reassure her that she's doing a great job. Reassure her that her children are beautiful, smart, and funny. Reassure her that you love those children and truly want them around. Above all, reassure her that you want her around, that her friendship matters to you. That, like all of us, is what she needs to hear.

Again, Hanging Out with Married People and Their Kids Season is a veritable smorgasbord of perks for single people. We get wisdom, laughter, kisses, and children who, as my friend Amy says, may adore us a lot more than our own ever will. After all, we're never going to take the car keys away from our goddaughter or tell our best friend's son that he can't date until he's in college.

Yes there will be nights when you sneak off to the bathroom because the sight of your friends bathing their newborn reduces you to tears, and there will be days when the last thing you want to hear about is the romantic anniversary weekend your best friend's husband has planned for her. There will also be sacrifices involved. You'll go to concerts less and the petting zoo more. You'll pass on buying the beautiful coffee table centerpiece from Pottery Barn because you know your godson will turn it into a weapon. You'll come to terms with the fact that most of your phone conversations with married friends will be punctuated by random instructions to "Stop hitting your sister!" or "Pull your pants up!" and come to an abrupt end with a loud cry followed by the words "Oh my God! I have to go."

But all those sacrifices really are worth it. They're worth it for the wisdom. They're worth it for the children. And, strangely enough, they're worth it for the deeper appreciation of the single years that friendships with married people often bring.

In the end, perhaps one of the most important lessons we can learn from married people is that the season we're in isn't such a sad season after all. Our married friends' lack of freedom helps us to be thankful for the freedom we do have. Their inability to take a weekend road trip on a moment's notice, make it regularly to daily Mass, or just sit quietly by a fire after work, reminds us to be grateful that we still possess the ability to do those things and more. Likewise, their sources of sorrow—miscarriages, children's serious illnesses, financial woes, and marital troubles—often make our own sorrows seem quite manageable in comparison. Our life may not be a walk in the park, but compared to the life of someone trapped in a bad marriage, it kind of is.

Knowing that does make surviving the single years easier. That is, it makes it easier most of the time. Some days, no matter how much our reason tells us otherwise, even the bad marriages look more appealing than going to bed alone. So what do we do then?

Ask the Single Girl

Dear Single Girl,

I turned thirty-four last week and am having a hard time not panicking. I've always wanted children, but it feels like with every birthday my chances for babies are slipping away. Do I just need to give up that dream?

—Childless in Chattanooga

Dear Childless,

I feel your pain. The clock is ticking. Sometimes, even more than not having a husband, it's not having babies that hurts. The husband, after all, can come along any time, but there's a limited window for little ones to make an appearance, a window that for many of us is rapidly closing. Don't panic, however. Chances are you have more time than you think.

What the culture doesn't tell you (but that you'll learn nonetheless if you spend enough time around non-contracepting Catholics) is that many women in their late thirties and early forties experience a fertility burst. They pass thirty-six and suddenly it's like they're in their early twenties again. Consider this the body's last desperate attempt to wring your fertility dry.

Case in point is my friend Lisa's mother, who had her first baby at thirty-five. Seven more children followed on his heels. Likewise, my friends Alicia, Marie, and Nellie have had four healthy, beautiful children each after the age of thirty-seven. My neighbor Ginna got pregnant with her fifth at forty-nine. Also, in Nellie's case, two of those kids were twins, which isn't surprising. Even without fertility drugs, our bodies' chances of conceiving multiples increase exponentially once we're past thirty-five. That little fact strikes fear in the hearts of my friends who already have large families, but I find it cause for rejoicing. "Twins" has become my new prayer.

Lastly, don't forget about adoption. My friend Amy was thirty-eight when she and her husband went through their first adoption. Over the next thirteen years they adopted three more children. Amy was fifty-one when their last little girl came home. Her husband was fifty-three.

I know adoption can be expensive. But not always. You can adopt for free (or almost free) through foster care. Likewise, at least at the time of this writing, the adoption tax credit seriously offsets the cost of many domestic adoptions. You'll also be surprised at all the ways people have found to afford international adoptions: refinancing their house, running a marathon to raise money, or simply saving hard while both spouses work.

The thing is, God always gives you the children you're meant to have. Sometimes those children come by way of your body. Sometimes by way of an airplane. They might even come by way of a future spouse's previous marriage. Whatever way they're meant to come, they'll come. If it's in his plan, God will provide the ways and means for you to have children, even if you don't marry until after forty. You just have to be open to how and when he wants to do that. That, not just refusing to contracept, is what openness to life is about.

Everything the Catholic Single Girl
Needs to Know About . . .
What to Do When It Hurts

It's a fact. Sometimes being single just plain stinks. No matter how fun and full your single years are, no matter how content you are with what God has given you, and no matter how slavishly you follow the advice laid out in this book, there will still be times when your single status is a thorn in your side. You can pray, work hard at a job you love, twirl in circles with toddlers, date only the right guys in only the right ways, philosophize about singlehood, femininity, and the culture, know the theology of the body like the back of your hand—you can do all that and there will still be days when you feel like Job: afflicted, persecuted, abandoned, alone.

That's normal. In fact, it's to be expected. Being alone when you want to be with somebody hurts. Being barren when you want to bring forth new life hurts. Being the one not yet chosen, not yet wanted, desired, treasured, loved, well, that hurts like hell. But that's part of the cross, our cross, that God has asked us to carry in this particular season of our life. It wouldn't be a cross if it didn't hurt, right?

Accordingly, the question for us isn't, "Will we hurt?" We know we will. The question is, "What do we do when we hurt?" When the pain comes, when we find ourselves wanting to do nothing more than crawl under our covers and weep, what antidotes do we pursue? How do we manage the sadness, frustration, and even anger? How do we deal with it?

The culture has some suggestions for us, but most of those aren't very advisable. Drowning our sorrows in ice cream or booze are short-term fixes that can lead to long-term problems. So is cozying up to some poor, unsuspecting fellow whom we have no intention of marrying or even dating. There's always my mother's go-to suggestion, "Stop being so picky." But you already know my feelings on that one.

Nope. Food, mood-altering chemicals, and sex won't solve our problems. Neither will abandoning our hopes, dreams, and principles. No matter how miserable we are now, we're on easy street compared to our sad sisters who've tried those remedies.

So what will work?

In ascending order, from somewhat helpful to most helpful, there's . . .

Retail Therapy

Okay, I'm sure with those two words my Catholic credibility just plummeted. But please, hear me out. I'm not talking about shopping 'til you drop, maxing out the credit card, or trying to fill the husband sized hole in your heart with a swanky pair of Pradas. And I did say we were moving up, not down, the helpful coping methods ladder. In all seriousness, however, a little retail therapy, used sparingly and always within one's budgetary constraints, can be quite consoling.

First of all, it's helpful because until you're a lot, lot holier, like St. Thérèse on her deathbed holy, you're still just a girl, which means a new skirt that swishes when you walk or a new sweater that brings out the blue in your eyes will make you feel prettier. And you need to feel prettier. You need to believe that you're beautiful, that the reason you're still single isn't because you're an ugly old hag, but rather because the general population of men have been made blind and delusional by the culture. Something new and pretty can help you believe just that . . . at least a little bit.

Second, retail therapy can be helpful because something new and pretty doesn't just help you feel prettier. It also, if chosen wisely, actually makes you prettier. The right dress or even headband can do a lot for a girl, and in the current marriage market, we need all the help we can get. As my friend Lindsay says, "You can't go fishing without some bait."

Finally, the reason you should buy that pearl grey silk dress for your night out at the symphony is because you can. Seriously. Ask one of your married friends. Most of them would give a minor appendage to be able to go out and buy something pretty for themselves. But they can't. They're buying diapers instead. Someday you'll most likely be buying diapers too. For most of us, the number of days we can spontaneously drop a hundred dollars on a dress will be limited. So take advantage of the days while they're here. They probably won't last. Then, when the blessed day comes that finds you clothed in sweats and covered with vomit and baby droppings, you'll be able to fondly recall the night that you were the best dressed woman in Heinz Hall.

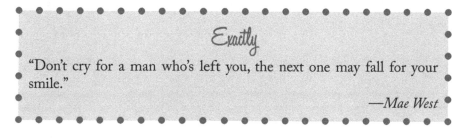

Exactly

"Don't cry for a man who's left you, the next one may fall for your smile."

—*Mae West*

Look Upon Beautiful Things

Even if you can't buy something pretty, you still can look. And I'm not just talking clothes here. Personally, a stroll through Anthropologie does cheer me up, but so does meandering through a museum, walking along a charming street, or thumbing through magazines in Barnes and Noble. God has made such a beautiful world for us and blessed us with the ability to add even more beauty to it. We're surrounded by beauty. It's the sea in which we swim, and it's not there to be ignored. It's there because we need it. Beauty heals. It consoles. It brings joy, and it brings wisdom. It's a window through which we see God. In every daffodil and Degas, there's something of him. So go look at him. Go look upon beauty on a trail, in a town, in Pottery Barn, and let beauty do its thing in you. It will help.

Make Something Beautiful

You're a woman, a member of the beautiful sex if you recall, and your nature is ordered to beauty—not just being beautiful or gazing upon the beautiful, but cultivating and creating the beautiful. You may not *yet* be able to create the most beautiful thing a woman can create—new life—but you can still knit a pretty blanket or sew some lovely pillows. You can paint a picture or (my preferred canvas) a wall. You can plant a garden, photograph ramshackle stairways built into the sides of hills, or bake a three-tiered lemon raspberry cake covered in homemade buttercream icing. If you're really depressed, you can take on a huge home renovation project. After one particularly crushing disappointment, I gutted my kitchen and remodeled the thing from the studs out. It helped.

Whatever you create, throw yourself into it. Have fun with it. Then, when you're done, take time to gaze upon it with unapologetic pride. If you do all that, you'll find that a good bit of your sadness fell by the wayside long ago, somewhere around the time you stopped thinking about all that you don't have and joined up with God as one of his co-creators, strewing the world with beauty.

Nine Shamelessly Secular (But Mighty Effective) Quick Fixes for a Bluesy Heart

- ◎ Pink tulips
- ◎ Radio sing-a-longs—loud ones
- ◎ Spring cleaning
- ◎ Kitchen dance parties (small children optional)
- ◎ A cozy fire
- ◎ A 2005 Bordeaux
- ◎ Swinging . . . the playground type
- ◎ Three words: Pumpkin Spice Latte
- ◎ An Agatha Christie mystery

Live the Life They Think You're Living

Fact: The number one reason most married couples you know aren't inviting you over for Friday night dinner is because they think you have something better going on. They believe you're living the high life, doing all the things they're convinced they would be doing if they weren't conducting a Disney Princess movie marathon in their basement. Prove them right.

Take advantage of this season with a long hot bubble bath and a glass of wine at night. Read for hours quietly by the fireside. Buy season tickets to the ballet or the symphony. Go to that Feist concert. Check out the new tapas restaurant downtown. Throw a fabulous dinner party. Sign up for the cooking class at the local Whole Foods. Learn to knit or sew or sail or whatever else you've always dreamed of doing. Above all, travel. See your friends and family scattered about the country. Drive to the ocean. Climb the mountain. Fly to Europe for a week every year. You don't have to be rich to see Paris in the springtime. One hundred and fifty bucks tucked away every month for twelve months is all it takes. Give up your daily Starbucks habit and you're practically there.

Like that grey silk dress, your time for these pleasures is limited. You can't fly to Europe while potty-training a three-year-old. You can't take long hot bubble baths when five other people share your bathroom. You can't pay for flying lessons when you're paying for piano lessons. Doing those things now, however, tempers depression in the short-term and enriches your life in the long-term. (Okay, maybe not the bubble baths, but everything else.) You see more and learn more. You grow more. All that will only serve to make you a better, wiser, happier wife and mother ... or single aunt and godmother. It also will ensure that all your married friends envy you about as much as you envy them.

Although, you really need to . . .

Stop Envying

First, because it's a sin. One of the deadly ones.

Second, because you may not know what you're envying.

Just like your single life is not the swinging, exciting roller coaster ride that your married friends think it is, the married life of all those couples you're wistfully envying is not what you think it is. That family of seven down the street? The wife almost left them all last year for another man. The adorable toddlers next to the mom with the newborn in her arms at Mass? The reason the dad isn't there is because he's serving a three-month jail sentence on a sex charge. Oh, and that newly married couple clasping hands in front of you at the grocery store. Tonight they're going to go home and have another knock down, drag out fight over the husband's online gambling addiction.

Those aren't extreme examples. Not in this culture. Nor are they hypothetical. They're real. All those couples are going or have gone through hell. But just to see them out and about, you'd never know. You almost never do. You can't know what's going on behind closed doors, often not even in the homes of your closest friends. You can't know about the tempers and temptations, the betrayals, the addictions, the breakdowns. You can't know how miserable and unhappy that beautiful mom with the beautiful children just might be. So don't envy her. Don't wish for what she has. There's a good chance you don't want it.

And no, not every marriage is an episode of the Jerry Springer Show. Far from it. Even the best marriages, however, have their problems. They've got cancer and depression. They've got kids who've left the faith, are sleeping around, or using drugs. They've got nothing in their bank account and in-laws who derive their greatest pleasure in life from rendering snide judgments on the decisions they've made. They've got toddlers who won't let them sleep at night, husbands who can't keep their travel schedules straight, and all of them want nothing more than to be able to go to the bathroom by themselves without their five-year-old walking in on them.

Remember: Marriage is hard. It can be beautiful, fun, glorious, and grand, but it always requires work. It requires dying to yourself so that you and someone else can get to heaven. That's a high-stakes game, so it's going to make its players sweat. If God calls you to it and makes it happen, he's also going to give you the grace to deal with the sweat. In the meantime, give thanks that you're not juggling a newborn baby and a husband with a sex addiction. Then go pour yourself a glass of wine and stare into the fire. In comparison to quite a few married women, your life is pretty darn good.

Count Your Blessings

Literally. Write them down. Tick them off on your fingers. Use an abacus. Enumerate them however you like, just count them. Count all of them. Your mind, your health, your strength, your friends, your faith, your beauty, your smile, your talents, your job, your lack of job, your wealth, your lack of wealth, your great family, your crazy family, blue skies, green grass, hot coffee, cashmere sweaters, fat babies, broccoli, old doors, new plumbing—whatever it is that floats your boat put it on the list. Then bless God for all of it. Thank him. Let him know you're not ungrateful. Tell him you see his goodness in all these things, and ask for the grace to see it in your single-ness too. Chances are, by the time you're done counting, you will.

Bodies, Blood, and Afternoon Tea

Sometimes, there's nothing like a good murder to cheer the feminine heart. So next time depression strikes, pour yourself a glass of wine, curl up in your favorite chair, and read one of these classic tales of sin and sleuthing. They are indubitably delightful and distracting, with not a tawdry sex scene in the bunch.

The Lord Peter Wimsey Mysteries, Dorothy Sayers
The Father Brown Mysteries, G.K. Chesterton
The Circular Staircase and *The Man in the Lower 10*,
    Mary Roberts Rinehart
The Miles Bredon Mysteries, Father Ronald Knox
Plus any and all of Agatha Christie's eighty-plus murderous
    masterpieces

Make a Gift of Yourself

All of us human beings—married, single, religious, consecrated—have one overarching obligation in this life: to give ourselves away in love to others. One of those "others" is always God. He wants us, body and soul. But it's not just God who's supposed to get us. Depending on our state in life, it's also supposed to be our spouse, our children, our parents, our friends, or the crazy old lady across the street. We're called to make a gift of our time, our energy, our talents, and our love to all those people in order to help them walk the long and often arduous path to God.

Jesus (not surprisingly) said it best: "For whoever would save his life will lose it, and whoever loses his life for my sake will find it" (Mt. 10:39). Those words don't just apply to martyrdom. They apply to how we live our life every day. So lose your life. Give it away. Volunteer at the local crisis pregnancy center one night a week. Sing in the church choir. Teach CCD. Feed the homeless. Take a meal to a new mom. Make a holy hour for the intentions of the singles you know. Be available for the 5:00 phone call from the friend in toddler hell. Smile at the crabby clerk in the grocery store.

Whatever you choose to do, do it often and do it gladly. God, as our mothers like to tell us, loves a cheerful giver. Accordingly, the more cheerfully we give ourselves away, the more joy, the more life, God gives back to us.

Go Have a Face to Face with Jesus

In the battle against the single girl blues, retail therapy and home renovations have their place, but when it really hurts, get yourself post haste to the nearest adoration chapel. Sure, you can stay home and shout at the crucifix or tell the picture of the Sacred Heart in your hall just how furious you are, but those are things. They're not Jesus. If you really want to have it out with him, go do it in person. Head straight for the monstrance.

True, if there are other people there you can't shout. But you probably shouldn't be shouting at Jesus anyhow. He is Lord of the universe after all. Plus he loves you and wants nothing but the best for you. He has a plan. Your singleness on this day, in this moment, is part of that plan. He's not surprised you're still single. He saw this day coming from all eternity. He's accounted for it. He's providing for you through it. And whether it lasts another month, another decade, or longer, he will continue to provide. Seeing him and being in his presence can remind you of that. It can also remind you of how much you love him, and how your deepest desire is not for a husband and family, but rather to do his will.

I'm not saying don't be honest with him. My guardian angel would start whispering "hypocrite" in my ear if I did. Also, it's not like God doesn't already know every angry thought you're thinking, so there's no sense in trying to hide those. Besides, you need to be honest with him. You need to tell him how you're hurting, why you're hurting, and what you would like him to do about it. That's a basic requirement of any relationship, and your relationship with God is no exception. He wants to be your most intimate confidant. Let him be that, and let him touch you with the very real, palpable graces that come from sitting in the same room as his Body.

If you do that, not only are you more likely to get the answers and the comfort you need, but you'll also start to recognize that although your pain is great indeed, in the grand scheme of crosses, you did not draw the short stick.

Which brings us to . . .

Single Sisters in History, Episode 4: Dorothy Day

In the eighty-three years she lived, Dorothy Day fell mightily from grace—aborting one child and conceiving another out of wedlock. But she repented just as mightily—first following God's call into the Catholic Church and then following his call to live a life dedicated to serving the poor.

As a suffragette, journalist, and founder of the Catholic Worker movement, Day challenged Americans to rethink what it meant to be a Christian. She also exemplified the feminine genius of passionate advocacy and care for the littlest and the least.

Dorothy Day knew sin. She knew tragedy. She knew poverty. She knew loss. But above all, she knew God. In her long single life, that is what made all the difference.

Offer It Up

I know. Most annoying words ever. Trusted fallback of Catholic moms everywhere. Abstract theological concept always easier to understand in theory than do in practice. Nevertheless, I got to say 'em, because it's your job—your assignment from On High.

God, you see, has this thing about not doing anything by himself. He always wants co-workers, people participating with him in his work of loving, running, and redeeming the world. Who knows why? It probably has something to do with him being a communion of Three Persons. God, by his very nature, doesn't do "alone." But regardless of why, he's really big on partnerships, and one of the main ways he's given us to partner with him in the redemption of the world is suffering. Paul makes that clear in Colossians 1:24: "Now I rejoice in my sufferings for your sake, and in my flesh I complete what is lacking in Christ's afflictions for the sake of his body, that is, the church."

Would it be nice if the main way we brought love and salvation to the universe were by picking daisies? Yes. It also would be nice, however, if God hadn't died a horrible, painful death on a cross. But he did. That's how awful sin is. That's the price he had to pay to buy us back from it, to redeem us.

When it comes to suffering for our salvation, God has already done the heavy lifting. But he asks those of us who love him and follow him to join him along the way of the cross, to pick up our sorrows—great and small—and willingly carry them so that we (and others) might find our way to the mansion he's prepared for us.

That's what offering it up is. It doesn't mean denying that your cross feels heavy or pretending like it doesn't hurt to hold. It simply means you don't run from it. You carry it. And as you carry it, you tell God it's okay, you'll carry it as long as he wants you to carry it because you recognize this is what's necessary and, eternally, best. If it helps, you can tell him you want the merits of your acceptance to benefit someone else, your friend whose marriage is in trouble or your aunt who's dying of cancer. Better yet, you can hand over all your merits to Mary, Mother and Mediatrix, to dispense as she, ever so perfectly, sees fit.

Don't worry, you don't have to smile while you do this. Nor do you have to think deeply and theologically about it. You don't even have to understand it. Sometimes, you don't have to do anything more than look at a crucifix and in the midst of tears say, "It's okay. It's okay. It's okay." God will always accept that offering, and before you know it, the tears will stop. You'll find the strength to get on with the day. And hope will work its way back into your heart.

Sit at the Foot of the Cross

When all else fails, when no comfort comes, don't despair. Just go to the Cross. Contemplate Christ's face, bruised and bloody. Contemplate his body, given for you. Contemplate his love, unwanted and rejected by the people he came to save. Look upon him on the Cross and sit with him there. Endure with him the hours when no comfort came, when the heavens were closed and the universe seemed bereft of grace. In that, know that you, mysteriously, are comforting him. You are his solace, his company, his companion in man's darkest moment.

I don't know how it works. You'll have to take this one up with God. But, somehow, just as the sacrifice of Calvary can be made present to us at each and every Mass, our love of Christ in his suffering can somehow be made present to him on Calvary. At least, that's what the mystics say. I like to think they're right. Because when nothing else helps, this does. The idea that my sitting with him in silent suffering comforts him, comforts me as well. If my being sad about being single somehow enables me to soothe one tiny milli-ounce of his pain, I'm okay with that. I'm actually more than okay with that. I'm glad for it. And if you try it, you might find you are as well.

Our Lady of Sorrows

Her heart was pierced by a sword. Go to her. She can help.

Most Holy and afflicted Virgin, Queen of Martyrs, you stood beneath the Cross, witnessing the agony of your dying Son. Look down with a mother's tenderness and have pity on me, who kneels before you to venerate your sufferings and to place my request with filial confidence in the sanctuary of your wounded heart. Present them, I beseech you, on my behalf, to Jesus Christ, through the merits of his own most sacred Passion and Death, together with your sufferings at the foot of the Cross; And through the united efficacy of both, obtain the grant of my present petition.

To whom shall I have recourse in my wants and miseries if not to you, O Mother of Mercy, who, having so deeply drunk of the chalice of your Son, and consoles with the sorrows of those who still sigh in the land of exile? O Holy Mary, whose soul was pierced by a sword of sorrow at the sight of the Passion of your Divine Son, intercede for me and obtain for me from Jesus (mention your request) *if it be for His Honor and Glory and the good of my soul. Amen.*

—Prayer in Honor of the Sorrows of the Blessed Virgin Mary

One last thought before we close this chapter out. Or, more accurately, a confession: I wasn't all that happy when I sat down to write these pages. Actually, I spent most of yesterday crying, telling Jesus how angry I was at him, and contemplating the shape of my spinsterhood. That usually involves resolving to sell my house, move back to my parent's hometown, and butter up the nieces so they'll take care of me in my old age.

In my defense, it's been a rough week. I've got one younger sister who'll be giving birth to her third baby in a few days and another younger sister who'll be getting married in a few weeks. I'm also planning my 954th baby shower for a former roommate, writing an article about the various romantic ways Catholic couples met, and contemplating my impending thirty-sixth birthday. Then there's this little book, which is fun, but let's just say being single long enough to be considered an expert on the topic was never one of my life's goals.

Like I said, rough week.

Needless to say, I wasn't exactly psyched about writing this chapter today. What I really wanted to do was go for a walk, put on something pretty, and make my way to Anthropologie for a little retail therapy. But like the good, responsible girl that I am, I settled down in my chair to type out these pages. First, however, I prayed my Rosary and read my devotional. And God, in his oh-so-funny way, had a message waiting for me there: Get over it.

Really, that's what he told me. In writing. The devotional reading for the day was all about a man walking through a forest and fretting about what perils he would encounter along the way. This same man had already been assured by a trusted friend that all would be well, that every need would be provided for, and sure protection granted against every trouble. But he fretted nonetheless.

So what did God, in the devotional, have to say to such behavior?

"I am with you to guide and help you . . . So leave your foolish fears, and follow Me, your Guide, and determinedly refuse to consider the problems of tomorrow. My message to you is, trust and wait.[1]

Trust and wait.

That's what this chapter boils down to: Trust and wait. In the end, that's all we can do. That, perhaps more than anything else, is our challenge and cross. But we're not alone in it. God is there now, and he always will be for as long as we faithfully walk the path laid out for us. That much we know.

And if it happens that we're walking down that path in vintage-inspired pink dresses from Anthropologie? Well, that's just all the better isn't it?

---

1 A.J. Russle, *God Calling* (Barbour: 1989). Entry dated March 26.

Everything the Catholic Single Girl
Needs to Know About . . .
Moving Forward

Before we wrap up this little survival guide, I have two summary pieces of advice for you.

The first I'm stealing from Dr. Janet Smith, the current grand dame of Catholic philosophy in America and one of the wisest Catholic single women around.

At the first national Theology of the Body Congress, held just outside Philadelphia in July 2010, Dr. Smith reminded the singles in the crowd that for the most part, singlehood was not something God was forcing upon us. Rather, she said, we've chosen it. We've chosen to put God and God's law first. We've chosen chastity over promiscuity. We've chosen our desire to have a faithful Catholic mate over just any mate. And all those choices have shrunk our pool of eligible spouses. We have fewer single men to choose from, and there are fewer single men by whom we want to be chosen.

But again, she reminded participants, that's our choice, and we need to recognize it as such.

Dr. Smith is right (as she is with most things). If all we wanted were marriage—any marriage to anyone—most of us would be married by now. Or we would be soon. If we were willing to widen the pool by forgetting about our faith, abandoning our morals, and lowering our standards, the majority of us could scare up some kind of spouse.

But that's not what we want. We don't want *a* spouse. We want the right spouse, a spouse who loves Christ, desires our ultimate good, and is capable of entering into a healthy, holy Catholic marriage. We want the kind of spouse God desires for us, and we know that anything less is not worth it. That's why we've made the choices we have, choices that have resulted in our current single state. Those have been our choices. God didn't force them upon us. We need to recognize that, and we need to own the choices we've made. They're good ones.

We also owe God some thanks for the grace he's given us to make those choices. Not everyone has had the same graces we've had. We are, as strange as it may seem, the lucky ones. We're the blessed ones.

So that's the first piece of parting advice: Recognize that your singleness is, at least in part, by choice, not just by chance.

The second is this: Stop borrowing trouble from tomorrow.

I say that, of course, as one of the world's greatest authorities on the practice. Like everyone, there are many things I'm bad at—math, sports that require depth perception, keeping my opinions to myself—and many things I'm good at—cooking risotto, hosting parties, charming small children. But there are only a few things at which I could be considered an undisputed expert. Borrowing trouble from tomorrow falls into the latter category.

Over the years, I've expended enormous amounts of energy fretting and fussing over one imaginary scenario after another—friends moving, airplanes crashing, my yet-to-be-conceived babies dying. Really, you name it, I've probably worried about it. The one fear that has wrung the most tears out of me, however, is the vision of my sad, lonely, old maidhood— me alone on Christmas, me wasting away in a nursing home, me in a solitary grave buried far from friends and family. It's a bit crazy, I know, but when I'm really down about being single, it's difficult to keep my mind from going there. One minute I'm crying because I have no babies, and the next minute I'm envisioning my half-eaten corpse covered in cats. As it so happens, the pain from that imaginary future vision is always a hundred times worse than the pain of not having babies right now. Not having babies makes me sad. The thought of dying alone makes me panic.

There's a reason for that, of course, a reason I'm getting better at remembering as the years go by.

Our God is a God of the present moment. He's with us now, in the day, and he gives the grace we need for the day. He gives us the grace to be alone today. He gives us the grace to be childless today. He gives us the grace to be single today. And that's it. Grace for the present sorrow, the present need, is all we get.

Tomorrow, when there's a new sorrow or a new need, he'll give us the grace to deal with that. If we choose to fret about it now, however, we're on our own. It will feel unmanageable and unbearable because it is unmanageable and unbearable. Grace and grace alone makes suffering endurable, and we're not yet being given the grace to be single or childless or alone tomorrow. We're being given the grace to be single, childless, and alone today.

So be in the day. When imaginary fears about the future rear their head, dismiss them. Ask God for the grace to deal with the problems on your plate *now*, to guide you *now*, to console you *now*. Likewise, remember that you don't know what the future holds. He does. He's planning for it. He's accounting for it. He's not going to abandon you to it. Again, trust.

Believe it or not, God does know what he's doing. He knew what he was doing when he made you to desire marriage. And he knows what he's doing now in permitting those desires to go unfulfilled for the present time. He could have made you differently. He could have worked in the events of your life and others' lives to make things turn out differently. But he didn't. He didn't because this way, for you, is the best of all possible ways.

On one level, I know that's stating the obvious. I also know, to most of us, it doesn't always feel obvious. It doesn't make sense why we—women who understand the truth about marriage, are open to life, and want to do the whole family thing God's way as opposed to the culture's way—are still single. It seems like such a waste—such a sad, tragic, needless waste.

But God doesn't see it that way. He sees our present singleness as part of a plan he has to lead us to his limitless love. He also sees our sorrows, accepted and joined to his, as the most precious gift we can give him, a gift he can in turn use to lead others to that same love.

We need to trust that he's doing that. We need to trust that he will do that. Even when we can't see or understand, we need to trust. It's one of the odd paradoxes of faith: Only in trusting what we can't see or understand, will we ever see or understand.

In truth, these single days of ours will never be a waste unless we choose to waste them. We get to decide if we waste the joys, the sorrows, the opportunities to grow and learn and serve. We get to decide what we do with this time we've been given. And as I keep saying, the time is limited. You and I may be single this day, this month, this year. But we won't necessarily be single next year or the year after that. One way or another, our single days will end. When they do, we don't want to look back with regret on all the grace-filled chances that we thumbed our noses at because we were too busy or too afraid or too close-minded to see them. We don't want to have missed all that God wanted to give us, because it wasn't what we wanted when we wanted it.

So trust, accept, buy yourself some pretty flowers, and know that God has great things in store for you. The fate he has for you is not a sorry one. It can't be. He's in it. He's part of it. He is it. You might not have the call to give your heart to God exclusively in this lifetime, but he's still the one you're meant to end up with in eternity. Which means he'll be there for you in time as well.

With him, you can survive anything. Even the single years.

Acknowledgments

If I'd been left to my own devices, this book never would have been written nor could it have been written. Fortunately for you (or unfortunately depending on your perspective), I wasn't left to my own devices. I had all sorts of help along the way and owe much thanks to many, starting with Shannon Hughes and Mike Sullivan of Emmaus Road for bamboozling me into writing this (and forcing me to sign a contract before I could change my mind). I also owe them and all the great folks at Emmaus Road thanks for their help in editing this book and getting it out the door.

In the months and years leading up to this book, *Our Sunday Visitor*, *Lay Witness*, *Franciscan Way*, and *Faith and Family* have all allowed me to research and refine my thinking about many of the ideas contained in these pages while still making some money. Small portions of chapters one, four, and six were adapted from articles published in those outlets, and credit is noted in the bibliographic essay that follows. Amy Roberts, Sarah Hayes, Shannon Walsh, and Theresa Wichert also deserve a big pat on the back for freely sharing their wisdom about the single life with me and for allowing me just as freely to pass it off as my own. This book would be much slimmer without their help.

Credit for all the pretty pictures and line drawings in *The Survival Guide* goes to Lindsay Carpenter, my favorite illustrator and one of the best married friends anyone could ask for. Lindsay, as well as Sarah Wear and Jessica Long, also deserve credit for talking me through this book and reminding me almost daily why I was writing it. Rob Corzine and Amy Roberts patiently read early drafts, and for their heresy checks and feedback, I shall be cooking them much risotto. Likewise Tom Crowe, Dave Mathews, and Chris Chapman have all heard more talk about a book for single women than any men should ever rightly have to hear and deserve more dinners than I will be able to make them. Thanks for your patience, guys.

Finally, in Rome last Christmas, shortly before I began the writing phase of this book, I knelt at the high altar in Santa Maria Sopra Minerva and placed this project in the hands of St. Catherine of Siena, who rests there. Along with St. Gianna, St. Teresa Benedicta (Edith Stein), the Blessed Mother, and the One Who Endures All My Fretting and Temper Tantrums, St. Catherine has been an invaluable aid in the completion of this book. The saints really do make splendid friends.

Bibliographic Essay

CHAPTER 1
Everything the Catholic Single Girl
Needs to Know About . . .
Vocations and the Single Life

If you're looking to learn more about the earliest Christians' understanding of celibacy and virginity, Peter Brown's *The Body and Society: Men, Women, and Sexual Renunciation in Early Christianity* (Columbia University: 1988) is your go-to source.

For general discussions on discernment, particularly pertaining to vocations, St. Francis DeSales' classic *Finding God's Will for You* (Sophia: 1998 edition) is an excellent place to start, as is Father Michael Scanlan's *What Does God Want* (Our Sunday Visitor: 1996). For an overview of the Ignatian process of discernment, I recommend Father Timothy Gallagher's *The Discernment of Spirits: An Ignatian Guide for Everyday Living* (Crossroad: 2005) and *Spiritual Consolation: An Ignatian Guide for Greater Discernment* (Crossroad: 2007).

To read more on specific vocations from the Church's perspective, the following magisterial documents are available on the Vatican's website (www.vatican.va): *Christifideles Laici*, On the Vocation and Mission of the Lay Faithful (John Paul II, 1988); *Familiaris Consortio*, On the Role of the Christian Family in the Modern World (John Paul II, 1988); *Casti Connubii*, On Christian Marriage (Pope Pius XI, 1930); *Redemptionis Donum*, On Men and Women Religious (John Paul II, 1984); *Pastores Dabo Vobis*: On the Priesthood and the Formation of Priests (John Paul II, 1992); *Sacerdotalis Caelibatus*, On Priestly Celibacy (Paul VI, 1967); *Vita Consecrata*, On the Consecrated Life (John Paul II, 1996). Also see the *Catechism of the Catholic Church*, nos. 914–933 (The Consecrated Life), 1536–1589 (The Sacrament of Holy Orders), 1601–1658 (The Sacrament of Matrimony), and 1716–1742 (Our Vocation to Beatitude and Man's Freedom).

For further discussion on whether or not the vocation to the single life exists, the following helpful articles are available online: "Is the Single Life a Vocation" by Mary Beth Bonnacci (http://www.catholicmom.com/catholic_match.htm); "The Single Vocation—Does it Exist?" (http://catholicexchange.com/2007/09/25/81229); and "Single State: Vocational

Limbo or Worth Cherishing" by Maria Wiering (http://www.catholicmatch. com/blog/2011/02/single-state-vocational-limbo-or-worth-cherishing/).

Finally, much of the original research for this chapter began with a series of articles I wrote on the single life and vocations for *Our Sunday Visitor* and Franciscan University's Youth Outreach Office. The articles on the single life were published on July 24, 2011 and are available online at www.osv.com. The articles on vocations were published in the Summer 2007 issue of *Fuel*, the official Steubenville Youth Conference magazine. Limited copies are still available on request through the University.

* * * * * * * * * * * * * * * * * * *

CHAPTER 2
Everything the Catholic Single Girl
Needs to Know About . . .
Who She Is and Who She's Called to Be

To explore the history of the Church's understanding of women, some of the best resources include Sister Prudence Allen's masterful two-volume treatise on *The Concept of Women* (Eerdmans: 1996, 2002) and Caroline Walker Bynum's books on women in the medieval Church, *Holy Feast and Holy Fast* (University of California: 1987) and *Fragmentation and Redemption* (Zone: 1992).

For a comprehensive understanding of the feminine genius, the two best sources, hands down, are Edith Stein's *Woman*, Volume II of her collected works (ICS Publications: 1987; now published as *Essays on Woman*) and Gertrude von le Fort's *The Eternal Woman* (Bruce: 1962). Also helpful are the essays collected in the compendium *The Church and Women* (Ignatius: 1998), as well as the books *The Privilege of Being a Woman* by Alice von Hildebrand (Veritas: 2002), *Are Women Human?* by Dorothy Sayers (Eerdmans: 1947), and *The Feminist Question: Feminist Theology in Light of Christian Tradition* by Father Francis Martin (Eerdmans: 1994). Although it's written from a Protestant perspective, John and Stasi Eldredge's *Captivating: Unveiling the Mystery of a Woman's Soul* (Thomas Nelson: 2005) is an excellent contemporary resource that is, for the most part, in line with Catholic teaching on women and very accessible.

The best magisterial sources on women are John Paul II's writings, his *Letter to Women* (1995) and *Mulieris Dignitatem* (On the Dignity and Vocation of Women, 1988), both available at www.vatican.va.

Many of the ideas from the above sources were explored in a series of columns I did for *Lay Witness* magazine in 2008, entitled "The Feminine Genius." Those are all available online at www.cuf.org.

* *

CHAPTER 3
Everything the Catholic Single Girl
Needs to Know About . . .
The Dos and Don'ts of Dating

For contemporary takes on the post-modern dating scene, try Dawn Eden's *The Thrill of the Chaste: Finding Fulfillment While Keeping Your Clothes On* (Thomas Nelson: 2006), Laura Sessions Stepp's *Unhooked: How Young Women Pursue Sex, Delay Love, and Lose Both* (Riverhead Books: 2007), Dr. Miriam Grossman's *Unprotected: A Campus Psychiatrist Reveals How Political Correctness In Her Profession Endangers Every Student* (Sentinel: 2006), and Kathleen Bogle's *Hooking Up: Sex, Relationships, and Dating on Campus* (NYU: 2008).

For a more Catholic approach, Amy and Leon Kass's book, *Wing to Wing and Oar to Oar: Readings on Courting and Marrying* (University of Notre Dame: 1999) contains numerous essays, most of which are excellent reading, that flesh out traditional notions of courtship and counter many modern attitudes on dating (although, notably, the Kasses are Jewish). Mary Beth Bonacci's *Real Love: The Ultimate Dating, Marriage, and Sex Question Book* (Ignatius: 1996) is an easy and helpful read, as is Father Thomas Morrow's *Christian Courtship in an Oversexed World* (Our Sunday Visitor: 2003) and Jason and Chrystalina Evert's *How to Find Your Soulmate Without Losing Your Soul* (Totus Tuus: 2011).

Although they have a strong Protestant flavor and are by no means perfect, Joshua Harris' books *I Kissed Dating Goodbye* (Multnomah: 2003) and *Boy Meets Girl: Say Hello to Courtship* (Multnomah: 2000) both have some helpful insights to offer from a male perspective on dating and courtship.

One of the newest Catholic dating books on the market is Amy Bonaccorso's *How to Get to I Do: A Dating Guide for Catholic Women* (Servant: 2010). Although I think Bonaccorso has lots of good things to say, she and I are of very different minds on some aspects of dating. Her book will be helpful for getting a different perspective from mine. Likewise, many years ago I read Steven Wood's *The ABC's of Choosing A Good Husband: How to Find and Marry a Great Guy* (Family Life Center: 2001). I remember it irritating me immensely. It's been years though, so perhaps my opinions would be different if I read it again. Regardless, different perspectives are good and you may find this more helpful than I did at the time.

* * * * * * * * * * * * * * * * * * * *

CHAPTER 4
Everything the Catholic Single Girl
Needs to Know About . . .
Sex, Chastity, and the Biological Clock

Although you should definitely read the actual text of John Paul II's catechesis on the theology of the body (preferably in the new corrected addition translated by Michael Waldstein and published by Pauline Books and Media in 2006), the subject matter is dense, so you may want to prime yourself with one of the many excellent introductions to the teachings, most notably Waldstein's introductory essay to the new translation. Another helpful aid would be the study guides by Mary Healy, *Men and Women are from Eden* (Servant Press: 2005) and Anastasia Northrup, *Freedom of the Gift* (Our Father's Will Communications).

For more on the basics of theology of the body, there is *Theology of the Body Made Simple* by Fr. Anthony Percy (Pauline: 2006); *Theology of the Body for Beginners*, Revised Edition, by Christopher West (Ascension Press: 2009); *Men, Women and the Mystery of Love: Practical Insights from John Paul II's Love and Responsibility* by Dr. Edward Sri (Servant Press: 2007); *Sex Au Natural* by Patrick Coffin (Emmaus Road: 2009); *Body and Gift* and *Purity of Heart* by Sam Torode (Philokalia Books: 2003, 2004)); and *Theology of His Body* and *Theology of Her Body* (Teens) by Jason Evert (Ascension: 2009).

If you want to go deeper, one of my personal favorites is *Crossing the Threshold of Love: A New Vision of Marriage* by Mary Shivanandan (Catholic University of America Press: 1999). *Discovering the Feminine Genius: Every Woman's Journey* by Katrina Zeno (Pauline: 2010) is excellent, and *The Christian Meaning of Human Sexuality* by Father Paul Quay (Ignatius: 1988) should be required reading for every Catholic (or for that matter every human being). Also, *At the Interface: Theology and Virtual Reality* by Sister Mary Timothy

Prokes, FSE (Fenestra Books: 2004) applies theology of the body principles in a fascinating manner to problems of virtual reality.

Precursors to the theology of the body that should also go on your reading list are Karol Wojtyla's (John Paul II) *Love and Responsibility* (Ignatius: 1993, revised edition), and Dietrich von Hildebrand's *Marriage: The Mystery of Faithful Love* (Longmans: 1929), *Man and Woman* (Logos: 1966) and *Purity: The Mystery of Christian Sexuality* (Franciscan University Press: 1989).

I also drew research and sidebar material for this chapter from the articles I've done on theology of the body for *Franciscan Way*, "Seven Things You Need to Know About the Theology of the Body" (Fall, 2007) and *Our Sunday Visitor*, "Making a Gift of Self: How John Paul II's Theology of the Body Can Help Catholics Better Live Out Their Vocations" (August 29, 2010); "Applying the Theology of the Body to Societal Problems" (September 26, 2010); "A Guide to Theology of the Body Resources" (October 24, 2010); and "Lost in Translation" (July 1, 2007).

* *

CHAPTER 5
Everything the Catholic Single Girl
Needs to Know About . . .
Being a Career Woman

To read more about the Church's insights into the feminine genius and work, both in and outside the home, the best places to start are, again, *Mulieris Dignatatem* and John Paul II's *Letter to Women*. Also helpful is John Paul II's 1996 Message for World Communications Day on "The Media: Modern Forum for Promoting the Role of Women in Society," and *Familiaris Consortio*.

Also excellent are essays by Edith Stein included in *Woman*, (now published as *Essays on Woman*) Volume II of her collected works: "The Ethos of Women's Professions," "Fundamental Principles of Women's Education," and "The Significance of Woman's Intrinsic Value in National Life."

To explore various viewpoints on the stay-at-home mom debates, books worth a read include *To Hell with All That: Loving and Loathing Our Inner Housewife* by Caitlin Flanagan (Little, Brown & Company: 2006); *The Price of Motherhood: Why the Most Important Job in the World is Still the Least Valued* by Ann Crittenden (Holt: 2002); *Stay Home, Stay Happy: 10 Secrets to Loving*

At-Home Motherhood by Rachel Campos-Duffy (Celebra: 2009); and *In Praise of Stay-at-Home Moms* by Dr. Laura Schlessinger (Harper: 2009).

Several contemporary Catholic writers have tackled the struggles of women to balance the need or pressure to work with the need or pressure to stay home. For further reading in this vein, see "Daze of Our Wives" by Beth Impson published in the January/February 2006 issue of *Touchstone;* Colleen Carroll Campbell's essay "A Skewed View of Stay-at-Home Motherhood," originally published in the *St. Louis Post-Dispatch* (October 8, 2009) and republished at CatholicEducation.org; and "The Bride Who was Groomed for a Career" by Lea Singh, originally published on Mercatornet.com, March 13, 2011.

⊛ ⊛

CHAPTER 6
Everything the Catholic Single Girl
Needs to Know About . . .
Married People and Their Children

If you actually want to read up on and study the drama of marriage, not just watch it unfold before your eyes, check out these classic works on the topic: *Marriage: The Mystery of Faithful Love* by Dietrich von Hildebrand (Sophia: 5th ed 1997); *By Love Refined: Letters to a Young Bride* by Alice von Hildebrand (Sophia: 1998); *Three to Get Married* by Archbishop Fulton Sheen (Society for the Propagation of the Faith: 1951); *Life-giving Love: Embracing God's Beautiful Design for Marriage* by Kimberly Hahn (Servant: 2002); and *Catholic For a Reason IV: Scripture and the Mystery of Marriage and Family Life* (Emmaus Road: 2007).

Church documents on the Sacrament of Marriage include: *The Catechism of the Catholic Church,* nos. 1601–1666, 2331–2400; the Second Vatican Council's Pastoral Constitution on the Church in the Modern World, *Gaudium et Spes* (1965, nos. 47–52); John Paul II's *Familiaris Consortio;* John Paul II's "Letter to Families" (1994); and Pope Pius XI's *Casti Connubii.*

For helpful insights into childrearing and family life, there's Kimberly Hahn's four volume series from St. Anthony Messenger Press: *Chosen and Cherished: Biblical Wisdom for Your Marriage* (2007), *Graced and Gifted: Biblical Wisdom for the Homemaker's Heart* (2008), *Beloved and Blessed:*

Biblical Wisdom for the Family Life (2010), and *Legacy of Love* (2011). Holly Pierlot's book for mothers, *A Mother's Rule of Life: How to Bring Order to Your Home and Peace to Your Soul* (Sophia: 2004) is excellent as is Lisa Hendey's *Handbook for Catholic Moms* (Ave Maria: 2010). I also highly recommend all of Meg Meeker's common-sense books on parenting: *Strong Fathers, Strong Daughters* (Ballantine: 2007), *Boys Should Be Boys: 7 Secrets to Raising Healthy Sons* (Ballantine: 2009), and *The 10 Habits of Happy Mothers: Reclaiming Our Passion, Purpose, and Sanity* (Ballantine: 2011).

Again, I also drew on some of my own research from an *Our Sunday Visitor* newsweekly series on the phenomena of Catholic divorce and the troubles afflicting Catholic marriages: "How No Fault Divorce Has Fractured U.S. Society" (April 26, 2009), "Should Couples Get Bishops' Permission to Separate" (May 24, 2009), "Exploring the Roots of Marital Infidelity" (September 24, 2009), "In Focus: Divorce" (May 22, 2011), as well as from articles on the dynamics of married/single friendships in the Advent 2006 issue of *Faith and Family,* "Friend of the Family" and the March/April 2011 issue of *Lay Witness,* "Bundles of Joy."

* *

CHAPTER 7
Everything the Catholic Single Girl
Needs to Know About . . .
What to Do When it Hurts

As far as I know, there are no magisterial writings urging single women to buy pink tulips. There are, however, Pope Benedict XVI's excellent encyclicals, *Spe Salvi,* On Christian Hope (2007) and *Deus Caritas Est,* God is Love (2005), both of which explore questions of suffering and sacrifice. There is also John Paul II's apostolic letter, *Salvifici Doloris,* On the Christian Meaning of Human Suffering (1984).

For non-magisterial writings on suffering, I highly recommend C.S Lewis' *The Problem of Pain* (Macmillan: 1944); Peter Kreeft's *Making Sense Out Of Suffering* (Charis: 1986); Father Michael Scanlan's *The Truth About Trouble: How Hard Times Can Draw You Closer to God* (St. Anthony Messenger: 2005); Scott Hahn's *Hope for Hard Times* (Our Sunday Visitor: 2009); and Mike Aquilina's *Why Me? When Bad Things Happen* (Our Sunday Visitor: 2009).

You likewise can never go wrong with these classic spiritual texts on the way of the cross: *Abandonment to Divine Providence* by Jean Pierre de Caussade, *Dark Night of the Soul* by St. John of the Cross, *Story of a Soul* by St. Therese of Lisieux, and *Diary of Saint Maria Faustina Kowalska: Divine Mercy in My Soul.*

I've also written more extensively on the Church's teaching on suffering, penance, and self-discipline in numerous *Our Sunday Visitor* articles, including: "When It Comes to Sacrifice, Mother Knows Best" (March 15, 2009), "Fasting Yields Multitude of Fruits" (February 24, 2008), and "Sacrifices of the Flesh" (February 24, 2010).

Emily Stimpson is a freelance Catholic writer based in Steubenville, OH.

A contributing editor to *Our Sunday Visitor Newsweekly* and a regular columnist for *Lay Witness*, her work has also appeared in *First Things*, *Touchstone*, *Franciscan Way*, *the National Catholic Register*, *Faith and Family* and elsewhere. Her writing has been honored by both the Catholic Press Association and the Associated Church Press, and was included in Loyola's Best Catholic Writing series.

Stimpson graduated from Miami University of Ohio in 1997 (*Phi Beta Kappa*, *summa cum laud*), where she studied political science, history, and English literature. She then went on to do graduate studies in political science at Johns Hopkins University and theology at Franciscan University. Before moving to Steubenville, Stimpson worked in Washington, DC, first as a Legislative Assistant to then Congressman Jim Talent (R-MO), then later at the Heritage Foundation, where she served as Special Assistant to former Attorney General Edwin Meese III.